SMILE LIKE A PIRATE!

FINDING HOPE IN LOSS

BRYAN DONIHUE

Edited by
LAURA HEWITT

For more information, send an email to:
bryan@bryandonihue.com

Stumped Publishing
a division of ADOS, LLC
Grand Rapids, Michigan

Second paperback edition, August 2020
First hardcover edition, August 2020

Cover Design and Layout by Bryan Donihue

Edited by Word Sojourner

CONTENTS

DEDICATION

First and foremost, this book is dedicated to Jesus, the Christ. He is the real source of Hope.

This book is dedicated to my wife, Christina, and my brood of kids. You've put up with many months of my unavailability while I was writing and many weekends where I am traveling to comic cons. Thank you for putting up with me and my obsession with telling stories.

For this book, I had an amazing editor, Laura Hewitt. Many authors might offer platitudes about their editors, but I have the best. This book would genuinely not be what it is

without her pushing me to delve deeper and push harder to be vulnerable while writing. Her guidance and help really allowed me to bring my story to you in the best way possible. Thank you, Laura!

I also had an amazing Beta Reader, David Cassiday. As an author, I rely on hand-picked readers to help me shape and hone the prose until it is perfect. David is an amazing Beta Reader and helped make sure this was as good as it could be.

I also want to dedicate this book to the amazing folks at Mary Free Bed Rehabilitation Hospital. You folks truly make a difference in lives everyday. I am happy to call Mary Free Bed my hospital, and I am thrilled to be able to work with you both for my own recovery, and to help provide some glimpse of hope for others.

Last, but certainly not least, I want to thank my family, friends, and Frontline Community Church family for all the support and hope you've provided over the last ten-plus years. This book is about finding hope amidst loss, and you helped me find mine.

KICKSTARTER BACKERS

This project was funded through a short-run Kickstarter campaign. These folks below were gracious enough to back this project. Thank You!

Kate Anderly

Carl & Carol Bicknell

David Cassiday

Shiela & Brian Dixon

Author Jay Erickson

Eulene Freeland

Christine Good-Deal

Paul Greenwald

John Griffin

Grace Hawthorne

Jessie

L Wray

C.T. Phipps

Connie Sattler

Bonnie Spaanstra

Danielle Thomas

Kathie Thompson

M. Eileen Widmer

Dianne Yonkers

INTRODUCTION

 I went to the woods because I wished to
live deliberately, to front only the essential
facts of life, and see if I could not learn
what it had to teach, and not, when I came
to die, discover that I had not lived.
Henry David Thoreau

On December 5th, 2018, my life changed.

After my fourth surgery in eighteen months, an
emergency surgery to clean out an infected joint, I had
to make a decision: go through another extensive knee
surgery and three months of recovery for a ten
percent chance of keeping my leg, or amputate my leg

above the knee and permanently get rid of the dangerous infection.

My wife, Chris, and I had already talked about this option, and we decided that I would have the amputation surgery. It was the safer, healthier choice. For the rest of that day I cried as the enormity of the situation hit me. I was losing a major portion of one of my legs, and was suffering a loss that would cause grief.

Fortunately, I had amazing support from the hospital staff, family, and friends as they comforted me in my grief. In fact, they surrounded me with care and comfort. As is the case in today's society, my social media feed blew up with condolences and prayers and commiseration. And this was all amazing. And eventually overwhelming.

Within a couple days, I had received so much support that I was feeling very overwhelmed. Part of my grief was turning to anger and frustration. As is my personality, I no longer wanted to cry. I wanted to laugh. I needed to laugh. My method of dealing with grief and anger was laughter. So I made a post on social media that said, "Thank you so much for the prayers and support... I've decided that I can either cry or laugh. So my social media is going to be funny. Sometimes really dark, but funny."

One of my favorite responses to my statement was made by a dear friend, Jannell. She said, "Is it too soon for pirate jokes?"

I genuinely laughed out loud when I read that statement. My immediate response was to say, "It's never too soon for pirate jokes - right, matey?!?!"

That became a turning point in my struggle to deal with grief and loss due to my new reality. This book recounts how I chose to work through my pain, finding joy in the process. It is about my choices while I reacted to the world around me. This book is about finding hope in a place of darkness and loss. It is about your choices as you react to the world around you. It is also about understanding grief. This book is to help you accept and work though your grief and loss when your life is going crazy. And it is about finding purpose in your life.

Why did I write a book like this? And why should you listen to anything I say? There are many books on these topics, and most of them are written by scholars, researchers, and famous people. I'm none of those. I'm just a minor author in Michigan who lost a leg to an infection.

This book is about personal discovery and a journal of my experience. It recounts some of the major difficulties I've had in my life, focusing in on my physical challenges with limb loss. As I have recounted my story to others, it has helped them, in some way, find perspective. So if I can help them, maybe I can help and encourage others. Maybe I can help and encourage you.

I am also a storyteller. My stories normally contain tales of fantastic beasts born of myth and legend, tales of heroes fighting the darkness of evil, and tales of dark monsters preying on innocence.

But this time, I get to tell my own story. I'll grant that there are not any monsters or evil beasts to be vanquished–although a particular x-ray tech supervisor comes close. But there is darkness, despair, and evil that threatened to overwhelm my real life. Instead, I get to share my tale of difficulty, of redemption, and of discovery. I hope this story, my story, is some form of help for you.

I want to help teach you to smile like a pirate.

NOTE:

I wanted to offer a couple quick notes here. First, This may not be the most politically correct book you pick up. I promise that I will not delve into politics or political issues at all, but I'm pretty blunt with my beliefs, and try to be scrupulously honest. My goal is never to simply offend someone, however, I might make bold claims in hopes of shaking someone awake.

Second, some small details may be omitted or changed slightly, and some names will be left out of my story. Nothing substantive is changed, but some details cannot be revealed without ripping away the protection of some folks in this story. Names that I mention are true, and I appreciate every one of them for helping me in this journey.

Finally, this book is unapologetically, unequivocally, Christian. It is my experience, my story, that God is very much alive, and is worth being worshipped and followed. Do I know everything? Nope. I already told you I am not a biblical scholar. Am I a "perfect Christian?" Again, no. I have never claimed to be perfect. Heck, I have the same struggles with which others contend. But I am forgiven and accepted. So God, the Bible, and Faith play a significant role in my life, and that may be evident in this book.

It is this point that I want to emphasize here. Finding true hope in the darkness, and choosing to live a life with purpose requires having, sensing, and living a higher calling. Difficulty, loss, and grief are a part of our life, and can easily turn into hopelessness. We have no choice over what happens in our lives. How we respond to those circumstances is ours to choose. I hope this book helps you find and choose hope.

CRASHING WAVES

> All the adversity I've had in my life, all my troubles and obstacles, have strengthened me... You may not realize it when it happens, but a kick in the teeth may be the best thing in the world for you.
>
> **Walt Disney**

I want to tell you that my life changed irrevocably on January 8, 2019. But in reality, it changed roughly ten years before that. January 2019 was just a course correction. Ten years earlier, in January of 2009, I slipped on ice and shattered my right femur. I later found out that a giant-cell tumor had eaten out the inside of my femur, coring it out like Swiss cheese and leaving it weakened.

I had just arrived home from a part-time job at a local gun store and had backed into the garage. While my normal job was a company that I co-owned, I had taken a part-time job to earn a little extra money, and the free range time was a bonus. It had been a cold, icy couple weeks in Michigan and I was tired from a long shift, and a long drive home. It was only my second day working that job, and my head was spinning with the information and new work procedures that I was learning.

When I backed into the garage, I noticed a mat that had slipped around and was sitting partially outside, right under where the garage door would come down. I got out of the truck and walked around to the front of my truck, intending to simply kick the mat back inside the garage and go inside. Instead, I slipped on a pool of ice that had formed right there, falling backward and slamming into the ground, smacking my head in the process.

When I finally looked around, I noticed that my leg and knee were sitting at an odd angle, propped up on the front bumper of the truck. I could not move them with my muscles, so, without thinking, I reached out and grabbed my pants shifting my leg back to where it should be. That was when the pain hit.

I screamed. Tears streaming down my face, I yelled

and screamed at the top of my lungs to get the attention of Chris, who was inside the house with our kids. My knee was on fire, with pain radiating up and down my leg. I was on my back, on the ice, with an icy drip from the eaves overhead landing on me steadily, and I was screaming at the top of my lungs for help.

Inside my house, the television and the kids drowned out my cries for help. Fortunately, one of my neighbors heard my cries and came to investigate. Once he saw what had happened, he quickly knocked on my door and got my wife to call the ambulance. As we were waiting for my wife to come outside, I realized that I was wearing a pistol on my belt. Chris does not like guns, and really did not know how to handle them. Even with the intense pain, I was trying to figure out what to do with the gun. I asked my neighbor to take the gun and lock it in my truck, out of the way and out of sight. My wife soon joined us with a blanket and said the ambulance was on the way. By that time, I was starting to feel the effects of hypothermia and shock.

Eventually the ambulance arrived, but they were unable to help me right away. Because I'm a larger guy, and because I had fallen on a large patch of ice, the EMTs needed additional help to lift me safely onto the stretcher. They called the police for assistance, and it was several minutes before that additional help came. By the time help arrived, I was wet, shivering, and in tremendous pain. I don't honestly know how long I laid there, the pain and the cold had sent me into shock.

The police department sent a couple officers to help, and they were able to lift me up to the stretcher. The pain was intense, driving me further into shock and numbness as I tried to stay conscious. Once I was in the ambulance, the short ride to the local hospital was filled with agony, and only slightly mitigated by the painkillers the EMTs administered. When we arrived at the hospital, the emergency room was overflowing. I was wheeled into the area beyond the front desk, and immediately assessed for triage. I was in agony and in the emergency room without my wife because she had to stay home until an emergency babysitter could appear. To make matters worse, all of the rooms in the ER were full, and several of the patients were triaged in the hallways. I was one more of those triaged to the hallways. The cacophony of the busy emergency room compounded my pain and confusion.

As I was being assessed for triage, the nurse administered more painkillers, and the edge was finally starting to come off the agony. Don't misunderstand, I was nowhere close to being comfortable. I was simply not whacked out with pain and agony. To assess my leg, one of the doctors started cutting my pants off, cutting straight up the leg from the bottom.

Odd memory time: I remember asking the doctor to not cut the shirt, because it was a brand new work shirt, and the only one that I had. When the doctor got about halfway up my leg with the scissors, I suddenly remembered that I was carrying a firearm in my pocket. Remember, I had just gotten home from my part-time job at a gun store. When I worked at the gun store, I carried my main firearm in a holster on my hip, and a second gun in my pocket. Somehow, I waded up through the pain and got the doctor's attention. I said, "You need to get one of your police officers. I have a gun in my pocket." The doctor took one look at the logo on my shirt and nodded, backing off and instructing a nurse to summon the hospital police.

By the time one of the hospital police officers responded, my wife had joined me. While I talk about the chaos and cacophony that is an over-full ER, it was a controlled chaos. Even though the emergency room was full, with patients triaged in the corridors, it was still a fairly quiet night. There were no disruptive patients, and certainly no one threatening anyone with a gun. Soon, a very confused hospital police officer walked into the corridor, looking around for whoever "had a gun" in the ER.

The second time the officer walked by, apparently looking for me, I called out to him that he was probably there to see me. Through the haze of the painkillers, which were blessedly taking affect by now,

I explained that I had my Concealed Pistol License and was currently carrying a firearm in the front pocket of my pants. I described what kind of gun it was, that it was in a pocket holster, and how to remove it. He carefully withdrew the pistol, keeping it in its holster and I let him know how to unload it. He said that he would keep the firearm in the hospital safe for when I was eventually released (I was able to pick it up later).

Once the pistol was taken care of, the doctor finally cut the rest of the way up and removed my pants. It was disturbingly apparent that my knee was absolutely mush. After a much larger dose of pain killers I was whisked off to x-ray. I was mercifully unconscious before I ever got out of the ER.

Upon seeing the x-rays, the doc told my wife that the lower fourth of my femur looked like gravel inside my knee. Think about that. The largest, strongest bone in the human body shattered into pieces that looked like gravel. And I had shifted them around by hand. It is no wonder that the pain was so extreme. I had rolled and shifted sharp bone shards around in an area that was full of nerves and nerve endings. Surgery was scheduled for early the next morning.

I say that my doc told my wife this information because I don't remember much after the initial ambulance ride. Other than the memory of the police officer taking possession of my little backup gun, I do not remember anything more at that hospital. I only became semi-conscious through a haze of pain at a hospital all the way across the state. Two days later.

SURGERY IN DETROIT

It turned out that when the first surgeon opened a small slit in the side of the knee to get a small sample of one of the bone fragments, he realized that the bone had been cored out by a tumor, and had promptly sewn my knee back up. Before the doctor was out of surgery, they were already making arrangements to move me across the state. They informed my wife that I needed to be seen by a specialist, and had contacted one of the two orthopedic oncologists in the state of Michigan. A short while later, they sent me by ambulance to Henry Ford Hospital. I went into a drug-induced sleep in Grand Rapids and (partially) woke up in Detroit.

Chris had quickly arranged for people to stay at our house and watch our kids, while she packed a small bag. She came to Detroit with a seven month old foster child we were watching. She knew that she would be staying for a while, and she made calls almost all the way over on the three hour ride, desperately trying to inform my family and hers, as well as arrange for other care for the kids she was leaving in Grand Rapids. By the time she got to Detroit, she had someone waiting at our house for the kids to get off the bus.

The first week at Henry Ford was filled with pain, sparse moments of lucidity, and a few odd memories. I sat for a week in the hospital bed with a shattered femur because the oncologist needed to make sure the tumor was benign. He told my wife and I that if the tests on the tumor came back that it was a malignant cancer, they would have to amputate my leg because they would never be able to make sure they got all the shattered bits.

Without being able to fix my leg, every test, every movement, and every moment was filled with agony. Morphine did not even touch the pain I was in, so the doctor put me on a Dilaudid pump with a constant drip. I also had a button that would inject extra pain killer into my IV as desired, within certain high limits. While I was awake, I constantly maxed out the injector. This brought me some relief, but also caused me to be only semi-conscious for the entire time.

SOME OF MY ODD MEMORIES—NOT NECESSARILY IN order:

At some point a few friends made the trip from Grand Rapids to Detroit to visit with me. I remember my sister-in-law caring for me while my wife drove three hours back home to get some rest and pack some clothes. My parents drove up from Ohio to help care for me, and then went on to Grand Rapids to help care for our five kids. And I remember a former pastor of mine visiting me in the hospital. In short, I remember a lot of really incredible, caring people.

I also remember other, not-so-pleasant bits. I remember being taken to another hospital by ambulance in sub-zero weather just so they could do an open-sided MRI. This required moving a still-shattered leg from my hospital bed, to the stretcher, an ambulance ride, moving from the stretcher to the MRI, and laying still for what seemed like hours.

I remember the pain, and maxing out my pain meds constantly to try to drive it back.

I have a memory of starving all day due to various tests, and finally going to the last one late at night–an x-ray. The supervisor was a smaller woman, and had evidently staffed the team with all her (female) friends that evening. We talked about the various methods to transfer me from the gurney to the x-ray slab. Once we decided to use the sheet I was on as a slide board, I gave explicit instructions of where to pull from and where NOT to push (big hint–don't push on the leg that was shattered). The supervisor herself pushed directly on the leg. I remember crying out and cussing. I remember a strong desire to physically deck the woman.

I also remember complaining about her to the nurse supervisor once I got back to the room.

I have a vague memory of asking for the tv to be turned to the Super Bowl that Sunday. I don't remember anything about the game, except maybe the Steelers played.

I remember the lemon ice desert. Due to many complications and the constant feed of pain killers, I was sick most of the time. I could not eat solid foods at all, and relied on liquids. Soups and juices were the diet for me, but my favorite part of every meal was the lemon ice desert. It was a small bit of heaven in a pain-filled hell.

A WEEK LATER, WE GOT NEWS THAT THE SAMPLE HAD tested as a benign giant-cell tumor. Why the delay? It had been tested at the hospital, but the tests were inconclusive, and the samples were sent to Harvard University Medical School. Harvard University determined that the tumor was, in fact, benign in nature, out to a 99% probability. Dr. Mott liked that number, and so we scheduled my surgery the following day.

The surgery was supposed to last about four hours. Instead, the surgery lasted more than twelve hours, due to the extensive damage to both the femur and the tibia, and also due to the sheer number of small shards of bone that had splintered. The surgeon was forced to remove a full third of my right femur, the top fourth of my right tibia, and replaced them with a shiny cobalt-chromium joint, with anchoring spikes up into my femur and down into the tibia. The doctor then put my original bone kneecap back in place and sewed me up, leaving a ten-inch long wound.

If you are interested to know what such a contraption looks like, the metal knee itself looked like the end of the femur. This was attached to a plate that was anchored to the top of my tibia with a hinge joint made of plastic. A normal knee does not actually have a hinge. The femur and tibia ride on a lining between them, supported by muscles and ligaments. A normal knee replacement simply caps the ends of the femur and tibia with metal, making sure bone-to-bone contact is not happening. My new knee was described as "more than a total knee replacement." The anchor spike in my femur reached almost up to my hip. Scanned images of the x-rays are included below.

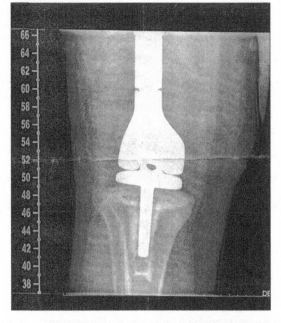

Front View X-Ray Closeup 2009

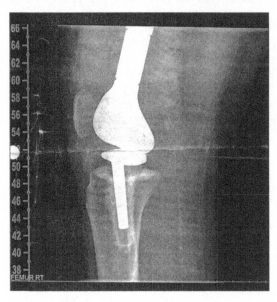

Side View X-Ray Closeup 2009

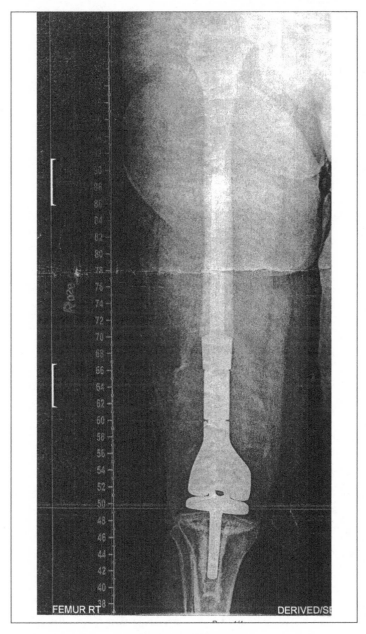

Right Leg X-Ray 2009

EYE OF THE STORM

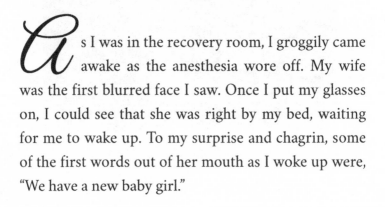

    You don't have to be a 'person of influence' to be influential. In fact, the most influential people in my life are probably not even aware of the things they've taught me.

Scott Adams

A s I was in the recovery room, I groggily came awake as the anesthesia wore off. My wife was the first blurred face I saw. Once I put my glasses on, I could see that she was right by my bed, waiting for me to wake up. To my surprise and chagrin, some of the first words out of her mouth as I woke up were, "We have a new baby girl."

My confused response was fairly glib for a brain addled with anesthesia and pain meds, "How long was I out?"

Her laugh was music to my ears, and she explained what she meant. She told me that she had received a call from the foster care agency where we were licensed. They had told her that they had a newborn that needed placement, and asked if we would take the little girl. She had agreed, and had arranged to pick up the new infant in a couple days.

All I knew was that she was not pregnant going into the surgery, and that she had announced a new infant when I woke up. This new one brought our brood up to six kids in the house.

The following week was another hazy time of gradually lessening pain, vague memories, more tests, and sleepless nights for my wife. Due to the trauma and surgery, I developed a blood clot called a DVT in that same leg. A deep vein thrombosis is a blood clot that forms in your larger veins-often in the legs or arms. The particular danger for a DVT is for the blood clot to break free and travel to your lungs. A pulmonary embolism in the lungs is horrifying, damaging to your lungs, and is often fatal.

The attending doctor recommended having a stent put in my upper thigh to make sure it did not break free and kill me. Once more I was wheeled into the OR for a brief surgery. The surgeon used a catheter to insert a small balloon to enlarge the vein. They then placed a small mesh filter and support inside the vein. After the surgery, I was taken back to my room with a new wound in the thigh and a hope that the blood clot would clear up. The prescribed blood thinners added one more med to the long list that I was taking.

I also ended up having to have three-and-a-half blood transfusions due to bleeding and other complications of the surgery and post-op recovery. My problem was that I kept blowing out veins in my arms.

Most of the accessible veins in my arms for blood tests, IVs, and transfusions are small, and buried deep under the skin. I can count on one hand the number of accessible veins in both arms, and that number includes the backs of both hands. So when a vein quits working, or I bend my arm wrong, or I have some other issue with the site of the IV, I have a steadily shrinking number of locations.

The last half-transfusion was supposed to be a full transfusion, and was only half a transfusion because it blew the last remaining good vein in my arms. Because we were nearing the end of my time in the hospital, we just hoped that I would not need an IV again.

Just over a week after the surgery, I was finally declared healthy enough to leave the hospital, and transferred to Mary Free Bed Rehabilitation Hospital in Grand Rapids for in-patient physical therapy. That trip was another interesting memory.

MARY FREE BED - TAKE ONE

It was early February and Michigan was deep in the throws of a cold, icy winter, and I had Mario Andretti as an ambulance driver for the 150 mile trip. The drive usually takes around three hours. We made it in under two and a half, while getting lost in downtown Grand Rapids.

If you have never had the pleasure of riding on one, ambulance gurneys are not comfortable for short trips. They are really not comfortable for a fluffy guy like me. Most importantly, they are definitely not comfortable on the broken, rough roads that are the result of Michigan winters and drivers.

I was strapped to a gurney, locked inside a rocket ship with lights and a siren, and hurtled across the state. When the bumps were bad, I was airborne. While strapped on a gurney. In pain. For over two hours. Mind you, the gurney was not airborne, it was securely locked down to the deck in the ambulance. I was airborne. Off the gurney. Every time I took off, the strap across my legs bit into my recovering right knee. When I landed, the jarring THUMP made every nerve ending in that knee shoot fire. I maxed out my allotted pain meds a half hour into the trip. It did not help.

About half an hour into the ride I braced my forearms underneath the rails of the stretcher and closed my eyes. I was pushing up with my hands and arms as hard as possible, just trying to stop flying off the gurney at every bump. I tried to drift off to sleep, but kept being jarred awake by being airborne off the stretcher. At those times I remember praying, "Dear God, if we wreck, take me quick." I was serious in my prayers.

Then the driver got lost in downtown Grand Rapids. I had to give the driver directions while facing backwards on a gurney and half whacked-out on pain meds. When the driver reached the top of the ramp at Wealthy Street on US 131, he turned right. I spoke to the EMT riding in back with me, "I think he went the wrong way. We should have turned the other way."

"You're facing backwards." The paramedic suggested. "You are probably just confused." Then he called to the driver, "Are you sure you know where you are going?" The driver was trying to follow directions from a printout of a popular internet mapping tool. He failed.

About five minutes later, the driver admitted he was lost and turned around, going back to the freeway, and then over the bridge. We shortly arrived at the front entrance of Mary Free Bed Rehabilitation

Hospital. Not the covered ambulance entrance, mind you. The exposed main entrance. Did I mention is was February in Michigan with sub-zero temperatures?

The short trip from the ambulance to the doors chilled me to the bone. We entered the main doors of the hospital and talked to a very confused-looking information volunteer. After calling someone on her radio, an admitting person found us and directed us to the right room. I was finally taken to my room and started a week of recovery and in-patient physical therapy in what would be a long battle with pain and recovery. My wife eventually made it to the hospital some two hours after I did.

Recovery and therapy at Mary Free Bed was unique at the time. It has changed since then, but I do not know if I would have the same outlook with the current procedures. While they are still one of the best rehab hospitals in the world, it still makes me sad to know that this one practice was completely lost by the wayside.

At the time, there were two scheduled physical therapy times at the hospital–one in the morning and one in the afternoon. All of the patients were taken to the therapy gym at the same time by the floor nurses. Then all of the therapists worked with their patients in that room or one of the adjoining rooms.

The first day of therapy surprised me when my nurse came to get me from the room and wheeled me down to the therapy gym. As they lined me up next to the other patients, it was like we were waiting to be picked for some horrendous joke of a neighborhood baseball game. On my right was usually a guy who fell off his roof and had lain in the snow for eight hours before someone had found him. He was now a quadriplegic. The woman to my left was a recent stroke victim who was learning to use her right arm and right side of her face again. Once she relearned how to use the right side of her body, she also had to learn to walk again.

I was there with a bum knee. No matter how bad my injury was, someone had it worse, and they were usually far more upbeat than I was. If the guy who fell off his roof could at least remain positive, how could I worry about a silly knee replacement? I'll grant you that this was not a conclusion I drew right away. It took me a couple days to figure it out. But when I did, that viewpoint made all the difference in the world.

That week was rough. When I left the hospital in Detroit, I could only bend my knee about ten degrees. Sitting in a chair normally requires about ninety degrees worth of movement in the knee–forming a right angle. Sitting on the floor, getting up from a fall, or even sitting criss-cross require at least one-hundred and twenty degrees of movement, if not more. Ten degrees of movement in the knee is basically no movement.

Why was I stuck like this? Because I had been unable to bend my knee and start therapy while in Detroit. For a normal knee replacement, the patient is on their feet within twelve hours of surgery, and starting basic physical therapy the next morning. I got to my feet precisely once after my surgery. That walk was a disastrous attempt at some sort of physical therapy. It also ripped open my wound some more, causing me to bleed.

Remember, in that week after the surgery, I had many complications, including the blood clot and the multiple transfusions. Because I could not move or get up and start working, all those muscles that had been damaged were now starting to scar over.

How do you break through the scarring and start to walk again? Painfully. It takes effort to bend the knee a bit at a time. It takes work to start using those muscles, and they are still recovering from the surgery. It also takes time. Pushing too hard, or actively forcing my knee and muscles to move risked the cobalt-chromium rod in my femur actually shattering through the bone. This would mean immediate pain and likely amputation. Rehab for a completely locked knee is hard, slow work.

Weight bearing exercises were combined with strengthening exercises. And those were added to movement exercises designed to give me more flexibility in the knee. This translated to pain. Hard work and pain.

There were many times in that first bit of physical therapy that I wanted to give up. Going from fairly active and moving to not even being able to stand up was demoralizing. The pain and work was tough. There was even a day that I just did not want to do physical therapy and I gave in to my melancholy and pain.

Times like this require hope that there will eventually be a good outcome to the process. Hope is the underlying foundation that allowed me to press on. When I wanted to give up, when I wanted to ignore the work that would get me better, and when I wanted to ignore the world around me, it was hope that brought me back. Hope reminded me that there were two major factors keeping me moving forward. The first factor was what I had discovered the first day of therapy–that my issues were relatively minor in the greater stretch of things. The second factor that kept me going through the pain, through the agony, and through the difficult work was the support of my family, friends, and church.

My family and I would not have survived without our family, friends, and church. And I would not be where I am today without my family. From the moment I was rushed down to the hospital after shattering my leg, all the way through my time in Mary

Free Bed, and beyond, my family was there to support me, our friends were there to support us, and our church was there to be the hands and feet of God.

While I spent a little over two weeks in Detroit, our friends and family were helping my wife Chris drop everything and come be at my side, three hours from home. Starting that first night, my wife made a panicked call to some family friends and arranged someone to come stay with our kids while she followed us to the hospital.

The next morning, when she found out they were sending me to Detroit, she called my family. My family lived in north central Ohio at the time, and my brother's wife, Jen, immediately left for Detroit to meet me there. While my wife made arrangements for someone to stay at the house to watch the kids while she was across the state, my sister-in-law met me at the hospital to make sure there was a friendly face there when I awoke. I vaguely remember seeing her there.

A family friend stayed at our house for several days while my wife was in Detroit with me. Simon was in high school when Chris and I moved to the area, and he and his family were basically family to us. Six years later, and having been one of our go-to babysitters for our special needs kids, Simon was a blessing as he stayed with the kids, getting them ready and off to school in the morning, and being there to care for them when they returned.

When my wife needed to go home to get clothing changes and to check on the kids, my mom drove up from Ohio to stay with me for a couple days. When my wife came back, my mom drove on to Grand Rapids to relieve Simon from babysitting duty. After my surgery, when Chris went home to get some more clothes, my mom remained in Grand Rapids for a while longer, eventually being relieved by Simon and his mom, Anne, as they alternated watching our kids until I came home.

Our family and friends weren't the only support we received. While we were away, my church had organized a food and freezer meal drive to help us get through this trying time. Chris told me that when she got home, she found our freezers stocked with a number of homemade freezer meals, as well as several sacks full of groceries sitting on the counter and filling the refrigerator. We were completely overwhelmed by this incredible display of support and caring.

Understand something, I had been a volunteer at my church in various ministry roles over the six plus years that we had attended our church. In that time, Frontline Community Church had grown from just about a hundred attending on Sunday to almost eight hundred, and had moved to a much larger building. I knew a lot of people, but I did not realize how many people I knew, and how many people cared for me until this time.

As a person, I have no problem giving everything I can to help someone, but I often have a hard time accepting help. I often don't know how to respond, other than to say, "Thank you." When my wife told me about all that our church had done, I broke down and cried in my room at Mary Free Bed.

These were not tears of pain or sorrow, but of joy, of thanks, and of some small inkling of what it was like to feel "church" happening. Between the realization that my injury was fairly minor in the grand scheme of things, and the revelation that we were a part of an amazing, awesome, generous church family, it was relatively easy to maintain a positive attitude during my hospital stay.

STUCK ON THE REEF

<blockquote>
" Sometimes life hits you in the head with a
brick. Don't lose faith.
Steve Jobs
</blockquote>

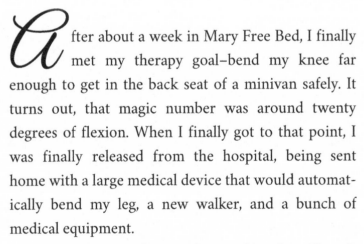

*A*fter about a week in Mary Free Bed, I finally
met my therapy goal–bend my knee far
enough to get in the back seat of a minivan safely. It
turns out, that magic number was around twenty
degrees of flexion. When I finally got to that point, I
was finally released from the hospital, being sent
home with a large medical device that would automatically bend my leg, a new walker, and a bunch of
medical equipment.

I want to pause here and marvel at that. First, it

took me a week to get ten degrees of flexion in my knee. It took us a week to break through enough scar tissue and start retraining muscles to wring another painful ten degrees of flex out of the knee. Second, simply adjusting the flexion by ten degrees allowed me to bend it enough to get in a vehicle. Ten degrees was the difference between the hospital and home. Small increments can make such a huge difference.

When I finally went home after weeks of surgery and therapy, I started a long road to recovery. Looking back on it now, the long rehabilitation time seems minor in the grand scheme of things, but at the time, it was earth shattering. Instead of being out and active, visiting prospective clients, my new normal spot during waking moments was laying on the couch. There I laid, my leg strapped to a machine that would automatically keep moving and flexing the knee. Because of the position that I had to be in to work with the machine, and because of the requirements for my therapy, I spent hours every day laying flat on my back staring at the television. These were the days before streaming services, so I was stuck with daytime television. Because of my position, I could not even use my laptop computer effectively. The one bright spot to this was that I got to bond with our new foster daughter from almost the moment I came home.

At the time, we had a seven month old little boy that we had been raising for his entire life. This little guy had traveled with Chris to the hospital in Detroit while she stayed with me, and was basically in Chris' care full time. Then Chris brought home this new little girl. Because the little boy was so well bonded with my wife, I was often tasked to hold, feed, and even change the newest little one. When she got cranky or fussy, it was my snuggles that would help soothe her to sleep. Colic? Daddy snuggles. It was soon evident that my "daddy" bond was far greater than her "mommy" bond, and that still maintains even to this day.

PHYSICAL THERAPY

When I first came home from the hospital, I began the tortuous process of in-home physical and occupational therapy. Most people understand that physical therapy is designed to help re-train your body back to some semblance of normalcy. Occupational therapy, for those who have not experienced it, is someone helping you remember, or figure out, how to accomplish basic, everyday tasks with whatever injury you suffer.

In my case, physical therapy was helping me figure out how to walk again, while working on exercises that would bend my knee a little bit further each day. The physical pain of physical therapy, when combined with the challenges of working out in a house, which was not designed for exercise, like a gym, meant new struggles. Unlike the daily interaction with the physical therapist at Mary Free Bed, the physical therapist was only at the house a couple times a week, which required even more self-motivation. Unless you are a very specific personality type, it is much harder to intentionally inflict real pain on yourself without someone driving you forward. At least it was for me.

Occupational therapy helped me figure out the basic everyday things with which I struggled. Tasks like putting on socks, getting up out of a chair, and standing in front of a counter to work on basic meal preparation were a few of the skills that I worked on during occupational therapy.

Putting on socks was one of the most challenging tasks that I faced in this new phase of my life. As a relatively fluffy guy, I am not the most flexible of people. When you can only bend your knee about twenty degrees, putting a sock on your foot becomes almost impossible. It is amazing how much frustration the simple act of putting a sock on a foot can cause. The attempt is even more frustrating when you wear compression socks, like I do. That frustration is compounded with the next small frustration, like having to learn to use a walker, and the next frustration, and so on.

One of the most intense feelings I had during that time after the hospital was an incredible sense of isolation. Not loneliness. Loneliness is the feeling of not being around people. I had people come over and visit occasionally. Although the frequency of the visits from friends slowed down significantly, I was still surrounded by family (now six kids, including two infants).

On the contrary, my feelings of isolation came from the lack of other patients, therapists and other medical personnel. I had been surrounded by doctors, nurses, and other patients for two weeks. Add the week of inpatient care at Mary Free Bed, and I had been surrounded by people who understood, on some level, what I was going through for almost a month. Then I went home. I struggled with this weird sense of isolation for a long while, and it really only lifted when I went back to Mary Free Bed for outpatient therapy. Even though I did everything possible to mask the pain and isolation, these feelings were a very real part of my life for months.

On the flip side, one blessing happened during inpatient therapy that we never expected. When I got out of Mary Free Bed that first time, I was sent home with a Continuous Passive Motion (CPM) machine. As mentioned earlier, this machine continuously moves your leg and knee, flexing and straightening the joint. When I left the hospital with it, I was told that the rental of the machine would be covered by my insurance.

In reality, the medical company actually had not checked with my insurance. They had assumed that since the use was covered for in-hospital use, it would be covered for outpatient use. This was not going to be the case. Fortunately for us, the medical equipment company realized that the mistake was their fault. The account manager that came to retrieve the CPM told me that the company had decided to waive the entire rental fee. This would have been upwards of three thousand dollars out of pocket, but the company decided to not fight the bill and waived the entire amount. I am still not sure how we could have paid that bill if they had not waived it.

Eventually I was healed enough, and prepared enough, to graduate from in-home therapy. The incision had healed and was able to be worked, and I was ready for outpatient therapy. This was the first time (but not the last time) I was introduced to the outpatient physical therapy staff from Mary Free Bed.

I was in physical therapy for over four long, painful months. Twice a week I was in the therapy gym. For the majority of that time, I worked with a physical therapist named Liz, and we got to know each other very well. She was the designated torturer, and I was the one consigned to be tortured.

I kid about the torturing, but Liz and the other therapists brought out the best in me. I worked hard. I worked to be able to walk without a walker. I used various exercise machines to gain muscle use and flexibility in my leg. And Liz worked as hard as she safely could to break some of the scar tissue down and help me gain flexion in my knee.

At that time, the outpatient physical therapy was in a separate building from the main hospital. The therapy gym was slightly smaller than it is now, and they had less equipment and a smaller staff. Regardless, they were still a world-class physical therapy department, and Liz was amazing to work with. I would work with her primarily, but would occasionally work with Brent if Liz was unavailable.

The hardest part for me came when I found out, twenty-five sessions in, that my insurance at the time did not cover outpatient physical therapy. Inpatient and in-home therapy was all covered, but outpatient was not covered. This meant that my therapy session, at $45 each, were costing me a small fortune. But I did not really have any other choice. I needed the therapy to get my feet back under me. So we bit the bullet and worked on it.

During this time, I was making semi-monthly trips to Detroit to follow up with my surgeon. My wife drove me three hours one way to visit Henry Ford Hospital to get checked up, and then three hours back to get home in time to get the kids off the bus from school. Every visit started with multiple x-rays, and ended with Dr. Mott measuring my progress as I bent my knee as hard as I could. Within a couple visits I had the pattern down, and was able to speed up the visits. Again, it was the little things that made the difference. I wore loose fitting shorts that were x-ray and exam friendly. I learned which poses Dr. Mott wanted to see when he ordered x-rays. And I tried to make the process as easy as possible.

I was incredibly happy when the good doctor finally judged my knee flexible enough to allow me to drive (I won't tell him that I was driving the week before that if you promise not to tell him).

One of the adjustments I had to make was to actually have my vehicle modified. I am a fairly tall guy, and I have always had issues with legroom in any vehicle I drive. That's why I drove an SUV. I loved my truck, and did not want to give it up. The company that worked on the modifications created custom seat rails, allowing my seat to move back an extra 2.5 inches.

What is 2.5 inches of legroom worth? Everything. This allowed my (long) legs to straighten out more, and meant that my knee did not have to bend nearly as sharply to control the accelerator and brake. That 2.5 inches translated to about fifteen degrees of less flexion required to comfortably manipulate the gas pedal and brake, and to quickly transition between the two. Liz and I spent time practicing moving between pedals and using the pedals to make sure I was safe on the road.

As an aside, let me help you understand what it felt like when I tried to bend my knee. To do this, I want you to do an experiment with me. But first, I think I need to clarify a couple terms. When I'm talking about the degree of flexion, or range of motion, it is measured in a VERY specific manner. It is the angle that the foreleg (your lower leg) bends, as measured from straight out. Straight out is considered zero degrees. The farther your knee can bend, and that the lower leg travels away from the flat zero, the angle goes up. Ninety degrees means your knee is bent perpendicular, and your lower leg is sticking straight down.

The angle itself is measured by a goniometer. This compass-looking device is placed along your femur, parallel with the femur and on the same level as your hip bone. The angle-measurement part is set where your knee is located, and then the second arm of this device is placed alongside your tibia in your lower leg. This sounds way more complicated than it really is, however it does take training get the measurements correct.

Now, we can do that experiment. First, bend your

knee as far as you can. For most people, the back of your thigh will come into contact with the back of your calf. If not, you will get close. This 120-140 degree movement is perfectly normal.

Now, sit in a chair where your foot is touching the ground, sitting somewhere around a ninety degree angle. Make sure the back of your calf is flat against the chair and your foot is on the floor. Now bend your knee further.

"But Bryan, I can't bend it further, my leg is already touching the chair."

I know. Now concentrate on the muscles in your knee. Flex them hard. Ignore the muscles in the rest of your leg, concentrate on the quads and knee itself. It is not moving is it? That is ALMOST what it felt like when I tried to bend my knee past wherever that current block was. I could concentrate and try until I burst a vein in my forehead, but the knee locked absolutely solid at a very specific angle. It was as if the cords of muscle inside the knee were permanently locked.

When I finally left outpatient therapy, I could bend my knee to about sixty-five degrees. And that was after a long warm up and a lot of heat to loosen up those muscles. Sixty-five degrees. If it was the temperature here in Michigan, that's a nice balmy spring day. Sitting down, sixty-five degrees means your foot sticks out in front of your chair by several inches.

How about we continue that experiment? First, sit back in the chair. Now, without holding onto anything, stand up. Easy, right? This time, stick your leg out at an angle that leaves about eighteen inches of space between the chair and your foot. This time, stand up without holding onto anything AND without moving that foot or bending that knee anymore. Not so easy now, is it?

One final trial. Kneel on the floor with both legs tucked under you. Now stand up, using nothing but the floor to prop against. It's perfectly fine to go to one knee, bending the other leg (usually your dominant leg) until it is able to be used to stand up–remember which leg you used to stand up. This final time, go back to one knee. The caveat? Your dominant leg cannot bend more than about sixty-five degrees at any time, and you cannot put much strain through it due to intense agony that will follow.

Dominant leg on the ground? Sure, now imagine the pain of your ligaments being crushed between the floor and metal, while never bending it more than sixty-five degrees (hint: Lean forward). Dominant leg at the angle and good knee on the ground? Sure. Except that you cannot get perpendicular to put enough balance through the leg to stand. And it is also really painful with all that pressure.

Sixty-five degrees. I lived with that for five long years. Five years of limitation and pain.

SHATTERED HULL

66 Hope is definitely not the same thing as optimism. It is not the conviction that something will turn out well, but the certainty that something makes sense, regardless of how it turns out.

Vaclav Havel

~

*O*h, the pain.

If you have ever walked into a doctor's office or hospital and complained about pain, they are going to ask you a question. "On a scale of one to ten, with one being none and ten being the worst pain imaginable, how would you rate your pain today?" My doctor's office had a helpful little chart showing a happy face at one and a crying face at ten, with a range in between.

The worst part about this scale is that it is subjective. The best part of this chart is that it is subjective–if you can explain your answer. What was my answer? For those five years, my pain was five or six on a good day and as high as eight on a really bad day. Daily. What was my scale? My ten was having my femur shattered into gravel, and then physically moving it and grinding all the bits together.

So how did I cope with pain on that scale? It was never drugs. In fact, other than some oxycodone only while I was in Mary Free Bed, I came out of the hospital and surgery drug free. This itself was a minor miracle due to the heavy doses of Dilaudid that I was on for two weeks. For those who are unaware, Dilaudid is a stronger pain medication than oxycodone, and is known to cause withdrawal symptoms after heavy use.

How heavy was my use while in Detroit? I maxed out the auto-injector every waking moment. My family doctor was amazed that I came out of the hospital without any withdrawal symptoms or an addiction to them. He had fully expected me to need to be weaned off of the meds.

If I was not using narcotics to handle the pain, how

was I surviving with such pain? By the grace of God and an incredible stubbornness. My body grew used to the pain, and when it got severe, I would take ibuprofen or some other anti-inflammatory. Always, I lived with the pain. This also meant that minor pains were easy to ignore, as they just became more background noise while I dealt with actual pain.

I also learned to mask that pain well. If someone has suffered tremendous pain for a long time, they often learn how to mask their pain. I became good at hiding the pain behind a mask. Even though I generally had a positive attitude, I also hid my pain as much as possible. Oh, sure, I did acknowledge my limitations, and occasionally admitted that I was in pain. At the same time, I worked hard to mask my pain behind a smile.

One of the worst parts of the post-operative life was when a weather front came through the area. Trust me on this, when you have over a foot and a half of cobalt-chromium inside your body, the slightest air pressure change will trigger pain. Believe me when I tell you that I was a better predictor of precipitation than the local meteorologist.

As I stated earlier, this deep pain lasted for over five years, until it became unbearable. That was when I had my second surgery on my right knee. In 2013, I was back at Mary Free Bed after having surgery for what I called my "10,000 mile check up and tire rotation."

During one of my semi-annual follow-up trips to Detroit, I asked the doctor about the worsening pain in my knee. By that point, it was becoming almost crippling, and there were many days that I was not able to walk more than a couple hundred feet without having to stop and collapse. After another battery of x-rays and other tests, Dr. Mott determined that I had developed a fair amount of osteoarthritic growth on the end of the femur, especially where the bone met the implant. This abnormal bone growth caused the severe pain and swelling as the femur grew layers of bone over top of the metal implant. The osteoarthritis had also begun on the one small bit of bone left in that knee–my kneecap/patella.

As we discussed the pain and the increasing stiffness, we talked about the options. It basically boiled down to two options: live with the pain or operate, again. We talked about the pros and cons, and he suggested that I should have the surgery to do a revision to the knee. Because he was opening the knee back up, he also decided to change out the plastic bearing that joined the femoral component to the tibial. The plan was to open up the knee, cut away as much of the osteoarthritic growth on the bones as possible, and then cut away some of the scar tissue that was blocking movement of the knee joint itself.

This would, in theory, free up much more range of motion for my knee and relieve a lot of the pain.

That surgery was supposed to be about an hour and a half long. It was actually four hours long. According to Dr. Mott, the scarring and osteoarthritic growth was far more prevalent than he first thought. This time, however, recovery was much more normal, and I was headed home within a couple days. The blessing here was that I did not need to spend time inpatient at Mary Free Bed.

A month of scheduled in-home physical and occupational therapy went exceptionally well. Two weeks into it, I was no longer using a walker, and we decided to end the in-home visits. Why the accelerated time frame? Two reasons. I got hit with loneliness and frustration of being cooped up in my house again. That led me to work harder at getting up and moving more. I spent more time trying to walk without the walker, instead moving to a cane for support. Once I was approved for outpatient therapy, I immediately started therapy once again choosing Mary Free Bed as the location. Due to Liz having a full schedule of patients, I chose to work with Brent again as my torturer, with occasional help from another physical therapist named Nicole.

I cannot stress how wonderful Brent and Nicole were for therapy. Neither one put up with any of my BS, and both worked me as hard as I could work, not as hard as I wanted to work. I worked hard while in the therapy gym, and worked equally hard outside the therapy gym to improve my movement and strength. The best part of this episode in my life came with the greater range of motion that I was able to get out of my knee. My proudest moment of all came when, after working hard during a therapy session, I was actually able to bend my knee to a full ninety degrees.

While it took an effort to get there, a maximum bend of ninety degrees meant my normal "resting" range of motion came in about eight-two or eighty-three degrees. Why did that make a difference? Remember the experiment earlier. My foot was effectively able to draw back to the chair. Going from stretched out foot and an inability to bend my knee to being able to sit in the minimum of a normal range made for an exponentially better quality of life for me. The joy of simply being able to sit normally was a glimmer of hope.

By the end of this round of outpatient physical therapy, I was able to walk around without a cane or assistive device, and able to bend my knee almost ninety degrees any time I wanted. While I still lived with pain due to cutting away the osteoarthritis, my quality of life was much better. In therapy, I had managed to get my knee to a ninety-five degree bend after doing everything possible to loosen it up.

None of that would have been possible without

Brent and Nicole. One of the recurring themes of this journey is the support of people around me. The support of Dr. Mott and the nursing staff that worked with him was priceless as I made my journey through surgery and recovery for both the first and second surgeries. When it came to working through the pain and re-learning how to function, the outpatient therapists and Mary Free Bed are second-to-none. Liz and Brent helped me learn to walk again after the first surgery. And Brent and Nicole really helped me recover from the second surgery, pushing me to exceed limitations of the recovery of the first surgery. Developing relationships with these folks helped keep my spirits up during recovery. That certainly made it easier to maintain my hope in the future.

Did the pain lessen? For a short time. In the end, I received a greater range of motion in my knee, which made a huge difference in my quality of life. I could participate in activities I had not been able to previously. Unfortunately, the pain returned a few months after the surgery, and eventually rose again to the same levels they had been prior to the revision surgery.

I just learned to live with pain. At least until August of 2017.

FROM BAD TO WORSE

That August, I had a routine dental exam, which eventually cost me my right leg.

How is that possible? No, I did not have a really bad dentist (she was actually pretty good). I learned a hard lesson that I am going to share here with you. If you have any type of metal deep in your body like a knee or hip replacement, pins or screws, or even a plate that helps support a broken bone, you should likely have a prophylactic course of antibiotics before and after any dental procedure.

Mind you, I'm not a doctor, nor do I even play one on TV, but my understanding, corroborated by my own experience, says that if an infection arises from this procedure, it tends to collect and hide where the metal meets bone in your body. What I did not realize then was that the blood vessels in the mouth are really close to the surface. This means that any dental procedure can cause an infection. Most people have no problem shrugging off this minor infection quickly, but those of us who are/were part cyborg carry an extra risk of the infection being able to hide out from the antibodies, and then start growing.

How do I know this? I am a living example. A few days after my appointment with the dentist, I developed more pain than normal in my right knee. Taking a few anti-inflammatories, I tried to work through the pain. My wife was away for the weekend with our two boys, so I was taking care of the four girls. In the span of a few hours, I went from pain in the knee to swelling and the inability to bear weight on it. I called my wife, and she cut short her trip with the boys to travel home.

I also called one of our favorite babysitters. Amanda came over to the house to watch the kids while I went to a local urgent care facility. In excruciating pain, I drove myself the couple blocks to the urgent care, and was able to see one of the residents. After some x-rays on the knee, the doctor was not sure what was causing it. On the x-rays it looked like the part of the implant that was in my tibia had come loose, and was potentially moving around as I walked. This would explain the pain and the swelling, but they were not sure about it. The doctor recommended that I go to the weekend orthopedic clinic run by the orthopedic surgical group for the hospital we use. There I could walk in and see one of the orthopedic surgeons to figure out what was going on.

My wife arrived home a couple hours after I got back from the urgent care. We talked about it, and she took me to the outpatient orthopedic clinic the following morning. When I was finally able to see the doctor, they took another battery of x-rays. When the doctor came in, he thought it might be an infection, or that it might be something else due to my medical history with the giant-cell tumor. He was stumped by the x-rays and the apparent lack of connection between the lower end of the prosthetic and my tibia, but he did not think it had come loose. I think the scariest part of that trip was finding out that the ortho doc had never seen an implant like mine. That did not fill me with a lot of confidence.

I don't know if you have ever been in that situation, but when a surgeon looks at the test result in an area that is supposed to be their speciality and says, "I don't know," it is a very scary situation. When I realized that I actually knew more about my implant than this ortho surgeon, I was scared. Add the pain and uncertainty of the situation, and my wife and I were very worried.

That doctor wisely referred me back to the lead surgeon in the practice. The new doctor was a much more experienced orthopedic surgeon in that practice. Unfortunately it would be two days before I could fit into his very busy schedule for follow up. When I was finally able to get in to see this doc a long two days later, the pain was severe and I was running a slight fever. When this new doctor came in, he took one look at my swollen, angry red knee and drew fluid out of it.

Instead of clear fluid or red blood, the fluid he drew was a yellowish-white color, cloudy and nasty. He did not even need to do any tests, he said that he was going to call and arrange to have me admitted into a hospital that afternoon. As he walked out the door to summon a nurse, he was on the phone with the hospital arranging a room for me, and a time for surgery the next day. Chris and I left his office and drove straight to the hospital. They were waiting to wheel me to my room when we arrived. That first infection surgery was the following day.

LEAKING LIFE BOAT

> Never succumb to the temptation of bitterness.
>
> **Martin Luther King, Jr.**

I was checked into the hospital very quickly. Once I was in my room, the nurse came in and got me settled with all of the routine hospital stuff. If you have not experienced being checked into a hospital, every hospital I have been in has the same practices. Once you are settled in your hospital bed, the nurse comes in to introduce themselves and make sure that you have everything you need. After taking your initial vital signs and connecting any necessary IV, they point out the tv remote, the bed controls for "comfort", and then talks about meals and food. They will then go over any medications you are assigned, ask if you need anything else, and then point out the call button to summon them.

A short while later one of the hospital administrators will come in to verify your information, figure out your insurance and how you are going to pay for your high-priced stay, and then you can finally rest. At least until the nurse or a nurse's aid arrives to take your vitals, give you your scheduled meds, or generally bother you. They will then leave you alone for a couple hours.

One of my memories of that trip to the hospital was trying to find a bed long enough for me. Not only am I a fluffy guy, but I'm also pretty tall (6'6" if I stand up straight). This means that normal hospital beds are far too short for me to use comfortably. This trip, because I was medically not supposed to stand up on my own, or bear any weight on my knee, I was officially labeled a "fall risk" by the hospital. This means that I got lots of extra attention to use the restroom, and had to have a bed alarm enabled. This was designed as a nanny, and if I got out of bed without a nurse around, an annoying alarm would sound, and a nurse could come help me or scold me–depending on the situation.

This time, the bed in the room that I was assigned

was a standard length bed (as most of them are). There is a way for most of those beds to remove the footboard and electronics, and replace it with an extension, adding over a foot of length to the bed. This sounds really easy, until the bed alarm on the extension does not work properly. As the nurse was standing there, trying to figure out how to set the bed alarm without it going off, I told her just to leave it off.

She argued with me, telling me that she had to have it turned on due to my "fall risk" status. I genuinely laughed at the irony as I promised to not get up from the bed without her permission. And then I pointed out to her that I literally could not stand to bear any weight on my knee anyway. I gave my most charming smile and promised to be a very good boy and stay in bed, asleep from all the pain meds. She eventually laughed and gave up. She said that if I did get up without calling her, she was going to stick the shorter footboard back on my bed to activate the alarm. That extension never did get fixed while I was in the hospital that trip.

Later that afternoon, the surgeon who admitted me to the hospital came by my room to talk about the surgery the next day. He told me that he could not personally do the surgery due to scheduling conflicts, but would instead have the other doctor do the washout. I will admit I was a bit apprehensive when it turned out that the surgeon who would be performing the washout was the same surgeon I had originally talked to. This was the same doctor who did not recognize my type of knee replacement hardware. After talking to both the referring surgeon and the one who was going to be performing the operation, I hesitantly agreed. I was told that this should be a simple procedure. The doctor would open the knee up, wash out as much of the infection as they could possibly find, and then pack the wound with even more targeted antibiotics.

In case you are wondering, the apparent gap between the lower end of my prosthetic and my tibia was not actually a loose fit. Dr. Mott had used a silicon-based cement to anchor both the proximal (upper) and distal (lower) ends of the prosthetic to the bones. This cement is clear to x-rays. He had to use a lot more of the cement on the lower connection, both for stability and for cushioning. This left an apparent gap of about three-quarters of an inch between the prosthetic and the tibia.

Why was I not seeing Dr. Mott in Detroit for this surgery? Insurance. The simple fact is that my insurance had changed, and that Dr. Mott was out of network for me. Since it had been over three years since I had seen him, my insurance would not cover the out-of-network expenses. This added to my apprehension. And I went into the surgery with deep concerns.

The surgery itself went well. The surgeon said that he had cleaned out as much of the infection as possible, both scraping it out and washing it out. He then packed the wound with concentrated antibiotic pellets before he sewed it up. He had even reused the original scar and wound area to make the incision.

Once I was out of the surgery, I was introduced to my new infectious disease doctor. I would get to know Dr. Simeunovic very well over the next two years. She was an amazing doctor, and worked with me extensively over the next two years as we dealt with this infection. We started talking about the antibiotics that I would be on for the foreseeable future. I was told that I would be on IV antibiotics for at least six weeks, and then would transition to oral antibiotics. The plan was for me to take the oral antibiotics indefinitely. Or until they stopped working.

Due to the extra care that was needed, I was assigned a visiting nurse for the time that I was on the IV antibiotics. I would also have in-home physical therapy for a short while, but the nurse I would see weekly. Molly ended up being my nurse for the entire eighteen months that I dealt with this infection.

The initial plan of IV antibiotics and nursing care was a great plan. Other issues unfortunately intervened. Shortly after leaving the hospital, I found out that I was allergic to the IV antibiotic that I was given. It was nowhere in my charts from before, and I had never been exposed to it. The week following my release, I was very sick. I could not eat anything. Everything that I ate or drank rapidly came back out. Even water made the return trip very quickly. I rapidly became very sick and dehydrated. I was incredibly weak and lethargic. And then my temperature spiked. Knowing that this was a sign of the infection causing issues, I was directed to the emergency room by my visiting nurse, Molly. Once my wife and I were there and checked in, I was taken into triage to check my vital signs and to place me in the queue to be seen. At this point, I was barely conscious, and largely unaware of my surroundings. When the ER nurse took my blood pressure, I was significantly below 90/60. I did not have to wait, I was immediately placed in a bed and started on IV fluids. I was able to return home that night after getting lots of fluids, and replacing the antibiotic with a different kind.

This surgery and the recovery period took far longer than I thought it would, and it nearly broke me. Due to the infection and surgery I was going to miss out on a very important convention for my business, and had the potential to miss many others. I was in a dark place in my life, and it was hard to see the end of the tunnel.

Grief and depression because I was going to miss a convention? Let me explain. I am an author and table-top roleplaying game designer. I have been in the board game / RPG industry for years. One of the biggest conventions that I try to attend every year, and that I had attended for seven years straight up until that point, was GenCon in Indianapolis. GenCon is the largest gaming convention in the United States, and consistently vies for the largest in the world. About 80,000 people descend on Indianapolis, Indiana for four days of gaming and in my case, networking with clients.

One of my clients is a company called Zombie Orpheus Entertainment. They make geek and gamer-related media. One of their biggest events of the year is a live improv show that they perform at GenCon every year. It is an amazing show, and not only are they clients, I'm also big fans of their work. Because I have worked with them for a while, I am friends with most of the folks in that company. This is legitimately something that I look forward to attending every year.

Because of my infection, surgery, and the resulting complications, I was unable to attend GenCon that year, even though I had planned several meetings with the folks from ZOE. Even worse for me, I had specially prepared some materials for Zombie Orpheus to use during their improv show. I was supposed to be traveling with one of my best friends, and we were going to have a great weekend at an amazing convention.

When I realized that my IV antibiotics and in-home nursing care were going to keep me from GenCon that year, I sunk deep into depression. Grief had reared its ugly head, and I was unprepared for it. Why did I grieve for missing a convention? I did not grieve simply because I missed GenCon. I grieved because an experience and tradition that had become a significant part of my life had been taken away from me. I did not make the choice to stay home. I was forced, against my will, to miss the trip. We experience loss and at least some measure of grief when we are forced by outside circumstances to break traditions. The more important, or more anticipated the tradition is, the more the loss or grief hurts us, affects us.

That was rough. And it was something that it took me a long time to get over. I shut it out and did not want to see what happened. In fact, ZOE live-streamed the improv show that year at GenCon, and I could not bear to watch it. It took me three months before I ever watched that show. Even then, the joy and laughter had an edge to them. To this day, I have never re-watched that particular show. That was truly the first real glimpse of medically-related grief that I suffered, even though I really did not recognize it at the time. It would also not be the last time I suffered grief.

What brought me through that grief? Over time I accepted that I had missed the convention. I just kept plugging away at life. I had to work my way through the grief, through the depression, and through the anger. I had to accept what had happened, I also had to find something to work toward. I had to get better because I had a couple more conventions coming up toward the end of the year.

Before I go much further, I want you to understand how IV antibiotics work, and why it would keep someone from really traveling at all. When antibiotics are fed directly into the vein, they work better and are more intense than oral antibiotics. This is often used for infections in the heart or in the bone, as these can become blood borne very quickly, turning septic and potentially deadly. Intravenous (IV) antibiotics are introduced to the veins through a PICC line.

If you have ever been in the hospital and had an IV, they usually connect to the one of the veins in the inside of the elbow. When the patient is going to be sent home with an IV, they need a PICC line installed. If the name "peripherally inserted central catheter" sounds scary and painful, it is. This is usually a small surgical procedure, requiring an ultrasound and other imaging equipment to get it right. The first time I had a PICC line introduced, I was taken to the OR (operating room) and laid flat on a table, with my arm strapped down.

After positioning the imaging equipment over the my arm and chest, the specially trained technician or physician assistant inserted a special flexible needle into my upper arm. Through this needle, they insert a long, thin, delicate catheter line all the way through my chest and into my heart, keeping it within the veins. At the outside end, there is a special sterile covering placed over the PICC line tube to make sure it stays sterile.

Why? Because it leads directly into my heart. Germs getting fed directly into the bloodstream via a PICC line will travel straight to the heart. This is an easy way to get a septic infection, quickly heading to a painful death.

When I was at home, I was supposed to hook up an IV bag once a day to this PICC line. This special bag of IV antibiotics was in the shape of a ball and was designed to slowly release its medicine over the course of twenty-four hours. This meant I was tethered to an IV twenty-four hours a day, seven days a week, for six weeks.

There was a special process that I had to follow when changing the IV bag. If I did not follow it carefully, the PICC line could become clogged, necessitating a trip to the ER and an emergency PICC line insertion, or I could introduce too much air into my line. Too much air in the line can cause an air embolism in my veins leading into my lungs or brain. An untreated air embolism is almost always fatal. I was trained to watch for air bubbles, and was told about what size they can become dangerous.

Every day, I changed my IV bag, often with the help of my wife. Once a week, my nurse would come and visit to change the sterile dressing around the PICC line, and to check and make sure that everything is ok. Molly was (and is) a great nurse, able to answer questions, and available to consult if anything unusual came up.

Not-So-Fun fact: When showering or bathing with a PICC line, you have to encase the entire area in a watertight covering so the sterile dressing does not get wet. Kitchen plastic cling wrap, secured with copious amounts of medical tape works amazingly well for a short shower. Of course, with a large open wound on my right leg, I had to wrap it in a watertight covering as well, covering the large incision completely. Trash bags work well, but tape on hairy skin is painful, especially in those sensitive areas.

The only times I was allowed to leave my house was to attend doctor's appointments or have lab tests run. After six weeks, I was declared fit enough to start on oral antibiotics. Molly came over and pulled the PICC line. It is weird, scary, and crazy to see over two feet of tubing come out of your arm, especially knowing that the one end had just been in your heart. Now that the PICC line was out, and the incision mostly healed, I could begin physical therapy again. Back to Mary Free Bed. Time to check in with Brent and Nicole. Again.

SHIPWRECK

66 Life is 10% what happens to you and 90%
how you react to it.
Charles R. Swindoll

~

That surgery started a cycle of surgery and
recovery that would last for eighteen
months and five separate surgeries–four of which
were emergency surgeries.

That first surgery was in August of 2017. Other
than the near-death experience of being allergic to an
IV antibiotic, I was doing ok, and was expecting to get
things mostly back to normal. The grief and depression was eventually dimmed and I got back toward an
even keel. Mostly. You see, I expected to live the rest of

my life with this infection. That meant that I would live the rest of my life on antibiotics.

This was the plan, at least until they stopped working. My infectious disease doc and I had a long discussion. The plan was to get me stable with the infection. I was going to use oral antibiotics for the rest of my life, or until they stopped working. I knew that if they ever stopped working, or if the MSSA infection ever became resistant and changed to MRSA, then I would likely have to have an amputation. At the time that was an "if" situation, not necessarily a "when" situation. With my church family praying for me, and the support of my family, I really believed that things would be ok. Until the end of January the following year.

MSSA? MRSA? WTF? The infection in my knee was *staphylococcus aureus*. MSSA is a methicillin-susceptible staph infection. This means that the bacteria is susceptible to penicillin-based antibiotics. MRSA is the methicillin-resistant staph aureus. MRSA is resistant to penicillin-based antibiotics, and was one of the first known so-called super-bugs. I was fortunate, I had the MSSA variant, which could be treated with antibiotics.

In late January, I went from the normal, everyday pain to a quickly worsening, crippling pain in that knee. Swelling and redness pretty quickly confirmed that the infection once again returned. The antibiotics were failing, and I went through another quick round of blood work to make sure the infection was still the same bug, and had not mutated. The infection had not become resistant, so in early February 2018, I again scheduled another wash out surgery. I couldn't help but wonder if the reason that first wash-out had failed was because the same doctor that did not know about the implant in my knee had performed that washout. Doubt was now a large part of my fears.

I have a history of using humor to move past grief and fear. It is my personality, my way of coping. Often dark, humor is my natural defense. As it became apparent that my first surgery had, for all intents and purposes, failed, it became harder and harder to mask my pain. I know that those who knew me best also knew that I was hurting, but I desperately tried to mask it to cover the grief and fear.

I was relieved to find out that I would have a different surgeon this time around. For this surgery, the doctor was going to be the same surgeon who originally diagnosed the infection. The same one that actually knew about my implant. In my mind, this time around should be better. At least this doctor knew what my implant actually was supposed to look like. If the previous doctor was second-string on the team, this surgeon was a starter. At least that was the hope.

This surgery was longer than the previous one.

This doctor spent more time cleaning out the wound to get as much of the loose infection as possible. He then packed as much time-release antibiotics in the incision as he could before sewing the wound closed.

Once again, I was on six weeks of IV antibiotics. This time, instead of the 24hr continuous drip, I had an IV infusion three times a day. This meant three times the risk of doing my own IV infusion. The plus side is that I did not have to wear a fanny pack with an IV infusion ball constantly, like with the first surgery. Molly was once again my visiting nurse, and things seemed to go well this time. When I came off the IV antibiotics, I ended up having an allergic reaction to the oral antibiotics that I was prescribed. Thankfully, it was not nearly as bad a reaction as the first time, we caught it quickly, and the new antibiotic seemed to work.

While I was recovering at home, I went through another bout of grief and anger at the situation. I had finally stabilized. Before this surgery I was back to working at the church. Through no fault of my own, the rug was pulled right out from under me again. Thankfully, because my infusions were different, I was able to work more, and keep my mind off of the isolation. I was getting more exposure to the outside world, and again, friends and family were a major support system.

This was two major emergency surgeries less than

six months apart. I am an author, and was in the middle of writing a different book for each surgery (books two and three of The Knight's Bane Trilogy). I need for you to understand how much these surgeries affected my writing and creative process. For an author, a clear mind is necessary to be able to coherently put together words and sentences to create vibrant stories. Creating an interesting, coherent story is critical, and not being able to concentrate due to pain becomes a problem very quickly.

After surgery, the pain and recovery process inhibited my writing process tremendously. What few pain meds I took also slowed down my creativity. It all affected my stories, my writing. For me as an author, not being able to tell my stories, to finish my books, was like a pressure building up inside my brain. I needed that outlet. Not only was being able to write my stories a release of the creative pressure that had built up, but it also acted as a catharsis, a coping mechanism for the pain and the fears. That may be why I wrote about monster hunting–there were some monsters in my own life that I could not hunt.

Thankfully, I was soon back at Mary Free Bed for outpatient physical therapy. Once again I worked with Brent for PT, with Nicole filling in when he was unavailable. Having developed these relationships with Brent and Nichole was absolutely vital to my recovery. Not just for their expertise, but for their caring support as they struggled with me through the disappointments and downtimes. In truth, I had learned most of the techniques already, but their presence, caring, and even friendship were much more important to my recovery.

I have another question for you. Do you have any idea what it is like to get your blood drawn every week or two for over a year? It sucked. First you walk into the all-too-soon familiar facility and greet the check in person with familiarity. Then get called back to sit in a chair that has become very familiar. Pick the vein that will be tapped this week, and then make small talk while you are stabbed with a needle (pain) and fill up the requisite number of test tubes. When you are done, smile and tell the technician that you will see them next week. The upside to this routine is that you soon find out where your accessible veins are located. The downside is that those veins get used and abused enough to make your arms look like track marks from IV drug use.

I had learned what the doctor was looking for in the test results, and watched them carefully. I knew when specific protein or enzyme levels were off, what the normal ranges were, and what constituted a dangerous reading. I even caught a particularly worrying level before I got a call from the doctor's office. I called them to talk about it, and we agreed on a course of action to correct the levels.

After the second emergency surgery, I could walk for some activities, but I was spending a lot more time in a wheelchair, especially for any kind of long distance. While I could technically walk and drive, longer walks or even trips to the supermarket would be spent in a wheelchair or scooter. With those limitations, I was able to attend a couple very important conventions for me, including that year's GenCon. Not only was I able to return to the convention after a rough year, it was also one of my best friend's 50th birthday, and David was inviting most of his family to join us at the con. GenCon was a tremendous experience, except that I had to see it from the seat of my wheelchair.

Cram 80,000 people into a convention hall that was about 300,000 square feet, with ten foot wide aisles. Now try to force your way through such a busy convention in a wheel chair. In a party of people that had two other wheelchairs in the group. Now add thick carpeting in the halls outside and in the aisles of the show floor. Do not come in from the parking garage, because there were only two working elevators, and they were VERY inconvenient to access.

Due to the limitations I was under, I was not only in a chair, I was in a chair with my foot sticking straight out in front of me with limited bending. I cannot tell you how many people did not see me, looked over me, or even stepped over my outstretched leg to get to some particular vendor display. There were a few times that I considered violence. Once or twice I even considered extreme violence, especially when a moron stepped over my chair and bumped my (very painful) leg to get to whatever hot knick-knack they were chasing.

Speaking of wheelchairs, the last 2+ years of medical issues have given me a newfound respect for anyone who is in a wheelchair for any length of time. It has also opened my eyes to some of the lunacy that is considered "handicap accessible" or "wheelchair friendly" in a business.

A wheelchair ramp set at forty-five degrees is not friendly, especially when there are no railings for going up or down (restaurant parking lot). Extra-thick padding may be nice to stand on or walk on in a convention hall for some folks, but try pushing a chair through it (I'm looking at you hotel on the west side of Indy).

Also, let us have a chat about bathroom doors that open inward, and are set in a small, narrow, hallway created by the privacy wall leading into the bathroom itself. Putting a door that way is NOT handicap-friendly, and installing a heavy spring to keep it closed lest we offend the masses with gasses is even less so (I had to wait for someone to hold the door to let me out - thanks again, same hotel on west side of Indy).

If you are a hotel or convention hall that holds

large events, EVERY damn bit of the event should be accessible without going outside the building and around the back (I'm really staring hard at you hotel in Richfield, Ohio).

I had attended a convention in July in Indianapolis, (see my comment about thick carpeting and bad bathroom designs above). After I came back, I was beginning to see the signs of the infection come back again. The orthopedic surgeon that had performed the last surgery took some new x-rays and performed a few tests and realized that he needed to refer me to an orthopedic oncologist who could handle my specific situation.

I was soon referred to Dr. Steensma. As an orthopedic oncologist, he had experience with medical histories such as mine, and had worked with implants like the chunk of metal in my leg. By the time I got in to see Dr. Steensma for the first time, my infectious disease doc had already switched antibiotics in a (vain) attempt to stop the resurgence of the infection.

GenCon 2018 was held in early August. With GenCon approaching and a couple very important conventions on the horizon, we talked about what the next steps would be. My new doctor and I talked over the possibilities and consulted with my infectious disease doctor to try to figure out how to stop this nasty bug once and for all. Our eventual solution was to remove the current knee replacement hardware and replace it with a specially-designed "spacer" that was loaded with antibiotics to hopefully get the infectious pockets that had become embedded in my femur.

This spacer, while metal, would not be nearly as stable as the knee hardware I currently had. The idea was that this new hardware would start working on the infection from the inside, while I went on another round of IV antibiotics for six more weeks. If the infection seemed to be gone, I would then be off of all antibiotics for another six weeks. If everything was still clear, the doctor would open me back up, pull out the spacer, and re-implant a completely new set of hardware. This should finally get rid of a VERY pesky infection.

Because the spacer was not nearly as stable as the standard hardware, I would be in a brace for the entire time after that surgery. No walking on my leg; I would have to be in a wheelchair and basically house-ridden for the full twelve weeks post surgery. If that all worked, then I would go through the other surgery, replacing the implant to a permanent knee replacement. And then I could finally start learning to walk again. Chance of success? I was assured by both Dr. Steensma and Dr. Simeunovic that they personally had always been successful with this type of surgery to get rid of an infection. The chances were nearly perfect. Nearly.

The new antibiotics appeared to be holding the

infection at bay temporarily, but we knew we would have to try the antibiotic spacer. With the convention schedule for that fall, we decided to wait until after GenCon and another convention where I was scheduled to appear. This would put the next surgery sometime around the beginning of October, right in between two different conventions. Because I was having severe difficulties currently, I was told to remain off my leg as much as possible before the surgery. This meant that I would be in a wheelchair for the vast majority of GenCon, as well as the other conventions that I was attending.

GenCon was bittersweet that year. Yes, I got to spend time with some amazing friends. Yes, I was able to hang out with some clients-turned-friends that I had not seen in a couple years. And yes, I was able to connect with some other friends and clients at GenCon. But attending in a wheelchair, with the limitations given, flat out sucked. From rude and pushy people bumping into me or stepping over me, to vendors who would not talk directly to me, and only talked to David, who was pushing me, I saw the convention from a very different point of view.

Side Note: If I have ever overlooked or treated anyone in a wheelchair badly, I apologize. I can tell you now that I will never treat anyone in a chair like that again. And yes, I have noticed how I have become more cognizant of folks in wheelchairs at conventions.

In the beginning of October, I went in to the surgical wing of the hospital for the third time in just over a year. After talking to Dr. Steensma and Dr. Simeunovic, I was in better spirits about this surgery. I had assurances that this was a solution that would cure the infection, and even allow me to get back to some sort of normal life. I was hopeful of a medical solution for the first time in a year, and I actually looked forward to the surgery.

The surgery went surprisingly well, and the doctor even let me keep the old hardware out of my knee. I was now stuck in a wheelchair for the next twelve weeks (three months). But I had a brand new paperweight for my desk.

FLOTSAM AND JETSAM

ope is being able to see that there is light despite all of the darkness.
Desmond Tutu

WITH A NEW PAPERWEIGHT FOR MY DESK, I HAVE TO tell you about the support from my church and my family and friends. I used to have a home office in the basement of my house. The rest of the basement was finished, but my office was painted and had a remnant over the bare concrete floor. It was not perfect, but I loved my office. It was big enough to fit a giant 10' x 4' conference table, a large L-shaped desk, and several bookshelves.

Being in a wheelchair for north of three months

put a damper on having my office in the basement. In truth, I had barely been down there over the last month, and would be unable to traverse the stairs for a long time afterward, if ever. We had to come up with a solution. In the end, we decided to finish off that room into a legal bedroom, and then move my office upstairs to the main floor. This would move three of our girls downstairs into a much larger room, and I would lose about a hundred square feet of office space.

A group of folks from the church, including a couple contractors, offered to help complete the trans-formation, as long as we were able to purchase the materials. They were also willing to help us remove the doorway to my new office so my wheelchair could fit through the door. In the days before my surgery, I helped as much as possible pack up years of tchotchkes and knick-knacks, over a thousand books (no exaggeration there), and shelves of boardgames and other assorted industry materials. In the end, I could only do so much, and one of the mens' bible study groups from the church came over and helped pack up the rest of my office. Before my surgery, my entire office was cleared, and work was ready to begin on the girls' new room.

Along with helping finish the girls room, my church came through in another amazing way for us. Shortly after I came home from surgery, I was told that they had raised enough help and materials to build a wheelchair ramp to the front door of my house. The gentleman heading the project had worked for other charities building ramps for houses, and therefore knew all the ADA and housing code rules that had to be followed. Even more of a blessing was the city engineer approving the plans on the first try, and approving the project that same day.

In a week and a half, in the middle of a real cold snap, the folks from my church had built a beautiful new wheelchair ramp, and it passed final inspection from the city the first time. In the weeks and months that followed, that ramp became vital to allowing me to get out of the house to go to doctor's appointments and other scheduled events.

One of the other blessings that we received, and that really helped out in and amongst all the craziness was the arrangements for meals from the church. When you have six kids and five of them are active in extracurricular activities, it becomes difficult for two parents to keep up. When one parent is no longer able to drive children around, having friends from the various activities able to drive your kids home is invaluable.

Having the church arrange to provide meals helped my wife juggle even more. When I was laid up and could not run and get kids from activities, or could not provide a meal for the evening, my wife, as most parents would, got overwhelmed. Meals from friends at the church were a real lifesaver during this time. This was important throughout the entire two years of this ordeal, not just after this surgery. In this, I have to give a special shout out to Angie, a dear friend of the family who is also the manager of a local restaurant. She occasionally went WAY beyond anything we could have asked for and delivered an entire meal for my family from the restaurant. Angie, you know who you are, and I thank you!

AFTER I CAME HOME FROM THE HOSPITAL, I WAS AGAIN paired with Molly as my visiting nurse. Once again I had IV infusions three times every day for six weeks. This time, instead of doing a full antibiotic drip bag over a two hour time frame, I was down to a slow IV push from a large syringe over five minutes, still pushing through yet another PICC line. This allowed me to be even more mobile, and really affected what I could do. Once again I was scrambling to get things done. As much as possible, I tried to get back to my normal schedule, while not being able to do anything normally.

After this surgery, there were some tremendous high points, and some incredible low points in my life. One of the highest points came that November. I was scheduled to be a Literary Guest at one of the largest comic cons in Michigan. I am an independent author, and had been publishing fiction for just about three years. I was not a large name in the industry, but I was getting a decent following in the West Michigan area. The owner of Grand Rapids Comic Con invited me to be a Literary Guest for the show that November, and I was excited to be offered the opportunity. This was a paid appearance, and would allow me to connect with new fans in a way I had never experienced. I also was going to get to meet some other amazing authors. The only down side is that I would have to take time out of the day a couple times to do a rapid IV infusion of antibiotics.

The experience was amazing, and I had a great day making new fans, chatting with some old ones, and having a seminar where over sixty people turned up to hear me talk about world-building for authors and game masters. With Grand Rapids Comic Con, Literary Guests are scheduled for only one day of attending, however they are allowed to attend (with upgraded Guest badges) the rest of the weekend. I was a Literary Guest on Friday, and was able to attend the con as a simple attendee the following day.

I have to pass on a sincere thank you to the security staff at GR Comic Con that year. In the middle of the day on Saturday, I needed to do another IV infusion of antibiotics. I had brought everything with me, but I needed an out of the way place to do the procedure. This meant hooking up a large syringe to the PICC line in my arm and letting it infuse. I did not want to do this in the middle of the con, for sanitary reasons, and also did not want to do it in a high-traffic bathroom for much the same reasons. I also genuinely did not want to do this in public because the last thing I needed to have was for someone to think I was openly doing drugs.

I approached a security guard with my medical needs and concerns, and she got her supervisor involved. Because I had a guest badge, and because I was polite and reasonable, the supervisor escorted me back to a secluded portion in the back of the show hall, and then stood watch for the seven minutes that it took to complete the whole process. This small kindness was an amazing kindness that I still cherish.

One of the lowest points of this entire process was my inability to attend and serve at my church. Other than the occasional missed Sunday due to vacation or job, I had not missed much of my church attendance in the past several years. Part of that is because I am one of the co-leaders of my church's safety team ministry. It was my ministry to volunteer at the church, and my joy to attend.

Once I had my surgery in October, I was consigned to a wheelchair, and not really supposed to be out and about much during that time. I had special dispensation to attend part of GR Comic Con due to my work, but attending weekly services became something far more than just a hassle. It was simply not able to be done.

I have an amazing team that works in the ministry, and had no fear that they were not up to the job. But I had infused Frontline Community Church into my DNA. As a follower of Christ, I look forward to attending weekly services. I also look forward to fulfilling my calling into that specific safety team ministry. And being unable do so drove me into fits of depression far more than missing a comic con or two.

This was all on me. In my head, I knew that what I was feeling was irrational. I was still following Christ, and would still go back to work in the ministry after all the surgeries. But being cut off from my church hurt deeply. I was cut off from friends that I had known for some sixteen years. Despite some of the amazing highs of being a guest at a major comic con, and despite other positives happening during this time, I was cut off from my church family. And it hurt. A lot. In the midst of my lowest point of being away from the church and isolated from society as a whole, I got terrible news.

As if foreshadowing what was to come, the final weeks of being on the IV antibiotics were painful and filled with setbacks. I had to have the nurse come out to clear my PICC line three times in the last two weeks. Why would I need that? When using an IV push for medication through a PICC line, the process is simple, but specific. First, the patient or nurse clears the PICC line with a syringe full of saline solution. Then the antibiotic is administered by connecting another syringe and slowly, over a specific time frame, pushing the medication into the line. This is followed by another syringe of saline solution to clear the medication from the line.

The final step is to connect a syringe of Heparin, which is an anti-clotting agent. This final syringe is supposed to keep the blood in and around the PICC line from clotting. If blood clots in or at the tip of the PICC line, then the PICC line no longer works, and the potential for the clot to break free and travel to the lungs is very high, and potentially deadly. If the clot cannot be cleared through medication, the patient must go into the hospital to have the PICC line removed and another one implanted. If a PICC line clots, it must be handled as soon as possible.

In my case, the first time my line clotted, I called the after hours nursing service. They sent a nurse out with a medication called Activase, which is a clot-buster. The nurse injected the Activase into the PICC line, and then we had to wait for about half an hour. Once the time was up, she was able to flush the line with saline satisfactorily. We completed that IV infusion and she was able to leave.

Less than a week later, about a week from my

scheduled end of antibiotics, my PICC line clotted again. Because this was during normal hours, Molly came out to the house. Once again, she used Activase and was able to clear the clot. I was beginning to wonder if I would have to replace the PICC line before I ended the course of antibiotics.

Just under a week later, for the third time in less than two weeks, my PICC line once again clotted and was blocked. I was one day from being done with the antibiotics. I literally had five more doses left (two that day and three the next). Once again I called Molly. Once again, she came out to the house, prepared to clear the line.

This time was different. The clot-busting drug failed to clear the line, and we had to make a decision. The nursing service called Dr. Simeunovic, and wondered if I needed to go get the PICC line replaced, or if we were complete enough with the course of antibiotics that we could simply stop the antibiotics and pull the clogged PICC line. I was risking the results of the surgery by not running the entire course of antibiotics, but it would have meant an entire procedure for just over a day's worth of antibiotics.

After impatiently waiting for a decision, the doctor's office finally let us know: I was ok to stop the antibiotics, and Molly was directed to pull the PICC line.

I was on the antibiotics for just shy of six weeks,

and all of the infection markers in my blood were down to pre-infection levels. After another battery of tests, it looked like the course of IV antibiotics and the massive nuclear blast of antibiotics from the implant seemed to have killed the infection. Dr. Simeunovic had cleared me for removal of all antibiotics. This was the first time in over a year that I would be free of any antibiotic medicine. I just had to wait another six weeks to make sure the infection was cleared.

Two weeks after I was off the antibiotics, I was scheduled to visit Dr. Steensma. I was supposed to have this final checkup, and then schedule the next procedure, which would be the one that would implant another permanent knee replacement prosthetic. We were looking at early February for the next procedure. Then the infection came back. With a vengeance.

On December 3rd, 2018, I was running a fever and was in pain. I had been feeling some pain in the knee most of the day, but was not really worried. And then I started to spike a fever. I went from minor pain to incredible agony and fever within a couple hours. With the spike in pain and the circumstances I was in, I called my infectious disease doc, and she told me to head to the ER.

At the ER I was in tremendous pain. Unfortunately, I could not take anything until they ran a couple tests. An ultrasound was up first to make sure I did not have a blood clot, and then a battery of x-rays, all made more cumbersome with a knee that was in agony and could not really be manipulated much. In the end, they were going to release me. I had an appointment with Dr. Steensma in two days anyways, and they figured that he would be a better follow-up. I thought there was something else lurking, but they could not find anything to keep me in the hospital. Until the nurse took one last blood draw.

When she did, she felt my arm. It was hot to the touch. She then took my temperature, which had originally been taken during intake. My temperature had spiked another degree and a half since I had started the evening in the ER. She went to see the emergency room attending doctor, and I was very quickly admitted.

The worst part about this bit was not that the doctor wouldn't listen to me about the pain, or that something was wrong. That was rough. For me, the worst part was the fact that I was not allowed anything more than a few ice chips until they decided to send me home. I was hungry. I was thirsty. And due to the nature of my complaints and background, they had to work on the assumption that I might need emergency surgery. This meant nothing to eat or drink. I was ready to kill for some Diet Pepsi (my personal drug of choice). By the time I was checked in, the regular hospital meal service was over for the evening. I ended up with a vending machine tuna salad sandwich and chips from David. And I finally got my pop. All just before the cut-off time for surgery the next morning.

On December 4th, I went into surgery. The agony was back, and my appointment with the good doctor switched to an operating room visit. To be honest, I do not remember much of that day after surgery. I remember talking to my wife about what was next. We both feared amputation. But we also talked about how long I had suffered with my leg up in a brace, with no weight bearing whatsoever. We talked about the timing of everything. We made a decision: Whatever Dr. Steensma recommended as the next step would be ok. Chris just had one request–if I was going to have my leg amputated, she wanted me to wait until after Christmas. Knowing I would be in the hospital for several weeks, she wanted to make sure we celebrated Christmas at home, and not in a hospital room.

I'll admit, I was devastated. I had hoped the infection was finally gone, and that I could go back to some sort of normal life. I was worried about what was next. Would I be in a brace for another three months? Or worse? I went to sleep that night with worry and doubt, and woke up with more of the same.

SINKING UNDER THE WAVES

> Tears are the silent language of grief.
> **Voltaire**

The following day, Dr. Steensma came in to follow up with my recovery. This was a conversation that I will never forget.

After examining my wound and talking about how the surgery went, he sat down and we talked about the future. We talked about possible reasons the antibiotic spacer failed, and the consequences of other treatments. We also talked about the vast number of different antibiotics that I had been on, and that I was quickly running out of effective options. And then we talked about what would happen if the infection went from MSSA to MRSA, the medically resistant form of a staph infection that does not respond to antibiotics. We talked about sepsis in the bloodstream, and the dangers it would pose.

When I asked him what the next steps would be, he told me we had two options. The first option would be to remove the current spacer and replace it with a new one. He would take even more time cleaning the wound, packing it full of antibiotics, and then place a brand new, antibiotic infused spacer. I would then be subjected to another six weeks of IV antibiotics. If the infection cleared again, we would then go for another six-to-eight weeks of me without any antibiotics to make sure we had truly gotten rid of the infection.

As with all options, this carried some pretty hefty risks and challenges. The first of which is that I would have to take another course of antibiotics for a couple weeks even before he could perform this surgery. This prophylactic course of meds would prepare my system for the shock of another spacer. Then he would swap out the spacer for another activated one. Once the new spacer was in for six weeks, I would be weaned off the antibiotics, again, and we would wait. Six to eight weeks. If everything was still clear at that point, he would remove the spacer and put a brand new artificial knee in my leg. When it was all done, the total time for this course of action was closer to four months. This would mean that I would have my knee immobilized for upwards of seven months, with no weight bearing allowed.

As we were talking about this, I was thinking about how I had already lost all definition in my right calf, and could feel the weakness setting in. I could not imagine how difficult re-learning to walk and move would be in another four months. Seven months of complete inactivity would be devastating to both legs, but even more so to the right leg.

I also thought about missing another four months of church and of serving. I would miss all of the spring and most of the summer conventions. And I would still live with tremendous pain for the rest of my life. While saving my leg was a good option, the future prospects looked daunting.

The other option was to amputate the right leg above the knee, removing about seventy-five percent of the femur. Why would he have to cut so high? The original knee replacement prosthetic had an anchoring spike that rose about two-thirds of the way up my femur. This cavity of bone had no marrow, and no way of growth, and would be weakened considerably by the loss of the cobalt-chromium rod. Because the cut would be so high, Any prosthetic I got would have to have a special system of harnesses to wear with connections wrapping around my waist.

The other, major downside of amputation would be that my life would immediately, irrevocably change.

I would have to relearn how to walk. I would deal with severe changes to my activities. And there was always the risk of me being stuck in a wheelchair for the rest of my life.

What would be the benefits of amputation? The largest one would be the removal of anything that might be infected. Getting rid of the metal inside my body would get rid of the hiding places for the infection. This would allow antibiotics to actually work as intended. I would be able to finally end my use of antibiotics. It would also alleviate the lingering knee pain I had dealt with for the past nine years.

I asked what the chances for success were for replacing the antibiotic spacer and living through four more months of wheelchair usage and downtime. Considering the results of this last implant, Dr. Steensma estimated that the chance of success for another antibiotic spacer would be around ten percent.

I was crushed.

Sitting with me in the hospital room, Dr. Steensma stressed to me that he would absolutely do another surgery if that was what I wanted. He could medically justify another attempt for the insurance company, and his office would absolutely try as much as possible to keep my leg. Part of me wonders now if this failure weighed on him more than he knew. He had told me that he had never been unsuccessful with the antibiotic spacer. Dr. Simeunovic had stated the same thing. Regardless, I knew he was giving it every shot he could. I thought long and hard about it, and then I asked him what he recommended.

Remember, my wife and I had already discussed this. We had talked about the various options, and some of the ramifications of amputation. Because she could not be there for this discussion, and because decisions had to be made, we had decided to agree to whatever the doctor would recommend.

Dr. Steensma was compassionate and I knew that he felt some of my pain when he delivered the bad news. He suggested that the more prudent option was to amputate my right leg. There it was. My doctor was recommending that I let him cut off the majority of my right leg. I was overwhelmed. Somehow, even talking about the possibility of amputation had not made that option real until that point in time.

Disappointment flooded my soul. I told Dr. Steensma that Chris and I had already talked about the options, and had decided to agree to whatever he recommended. Reluctantly, hesitantly, and numb with shock, I agreed that we should do the amputation.

I told the doctor that my wife's one request was that we hold off the surgery until after Christmas. Because that would give me more time to be on antibiotics, the doctor agreed. Surgery would soon be tentatively scheduled for December 26, 2018. The day after Christmas.

GRIEF

I cried.

As soon as the doctor left my room, I lost any composure I had. Tears welled up in my eyes. Everything that we decided hit me like a ton of bricks. I just agreed that I would voluntarily let the doctor cut off the majority of my right leg. My life would forever be altered.

Would I ever walk again? Would I ever be able to spend time outside with my kids? These questions, and others, rattled around in my skull like ping pong balls in a lottery machine. Unfortunately my numbers were coming up as losers. This was, until then, the worst moment of grief I had ever felt. It was the most real. I had attended the funerals of loved ones and friends, but this was somehow more devastating. I tearfully typed out a brief message to my wife and my parents on my phone. I knew there was no way I could talk without completely breaking down. Well, breaking down any more than I already had.

One of the duty nurses came in soon after the doctor left to see how I was doing, and immediately saw that I was broken. Judy did one of the best things that anyone could have done for me at that time. She sat with me. She didn't say anything comforting. She did not try to soothe my emotions. She did not try to walk me through the steps to grief. She sat with me. She sat in my room for the next couple hours. The only time she left my room was when another of her patients needed something, otherwise, she stayed with me. She had another nurse carry out her rounds.

When I was able to talk, she talked with me. When I could not talk, and just sobbed, Judy grieved with me. As a "macho man who doesn't much cry", it took me a long time before I could halt the flow of tears. Her presence, her silent caring, and her sharing of my pain was far more of what I needed at that point. I found comfort in her caring presence. She also reflected another caring presence that I did not recognize at the time.

During one of the times Judy had to step out of the room, she searched out someone who would become very important in my new life. Even though it was part of a different medical group, Mary Free Bed had a small office in the orthopedic wing of Spectrum Hospital. Their Amputee Care Liaison can occasionally be found in this office, and if not, she is always available for a call from the hospital. Stephanie soon came to visit me, introducing herself and her position for Mary Free Bed. She told me that she helped amputees make the transition to their new lives. Before I left Spectrum, Stephanie already had me registered in the system as an incoming amputee at Mary Free Bed. I knew that I would be working with Dr. Bruinsma, the head of the amputee department.

I finally got that initial swell of emotion under control, keeping my tears in check, at least until my wife arrived. When Chris arrived, my tears flowed heavily again. Soon after, Judy's shift ended, and I never saw Judy again while I was in Spectrum. She was not scheduled to cover my floor again until after I was released. I regret that she will never know how much help she was to me.

I spent the next day or so wallowing in grief. As members of today's modern society, my wife and I had reached out to friends and family on social media to inform them of the situation. Sharing such pain can be cathartic, or it can make the situation worse. I had received calls from my family, calls from my pastors, and visits from friends. On social media, I had a staggering outpouring of support from friends all over the United States, and even a couple from overseas. Unfortunately for me, the sheer volume of condolences and well-wishes was overwhelming.

After the last couple days, I was tired of swimming in the muck that is grief. Part of my grief was turning to anger and frustration. I was still angry and resentful that I was going to go through all of this. I was also frustrated. After all, I was one who often comforted people. I was one who tried my darnedest to cheer people up, or to help get them past depression. I wasn't one who had to be comforted. I legitimately did not know how to be comforted by others.

One of my coping mechanisms for bad news, rough emotions, and other crap is to find some small humor. I have spent years as a first responder, so I learned to cover my horror or dark feelings with a dark sense of humor. This is a coping mechanism found in a lot of first responders and military personnel.

Want an example? Most civilians are taught to perform CPR chest compressions to the tune of "Stayin' Alive" by the Bee Gees. It's a nice upbeat song at about a hundred beats per minute. Law enforcement or paramedics? I've trained them with "Another One Bites The Dust" by Queen. It's also about a hundred beats per minute. If I'm teaching first responders who are country fans? "Achey Breaky Heart" by Billy Ray Cyrus fits the bill. Dark humor is a way of helping your mind adjust to all-too-real horrors in the real world. It's a way of coping. And it can mask the pain.

The short of it was that I no longer wanted to cry. I wanted to laugh. I needed to laugh. My method of dealing with grief and anger was laughter. Oh, the grief was still there. The anger never left. But I needed laughter to cope. So I made a post on social media that said something to the effect of, "Thank you for all of the prayers and condolences. But I want to laugh. Please fill my feed with jokes, funny stories, and memes. And yes, amputee jokes are fine."

One of my favorite responses to my statement was made by a dear friend, Jannell. She said, "Question..... is it too soon for pirate jokes? Because you could come out to the marina and hang out on our boat, we would be the envy of the marina to have our very own pirate."

When I read that, I laughed out loud. My response was "It's never too soon for pirate jokes - right, matey?!?!" I told you, dark sense of humor.

From then on, I tried desperately to be positive. I posted jokes and laughed with friends. And inside I was scared and still grieving. I did not know what the future would hold for me. And that scared the crap out of me. You need to know, this is absolutely normal for any major surgery, let alone an amputation. Being scared and grieving are normal. It does not make it suck any less, though.

The day I made a decision to laugh, I got a roommate in my hospital room. This gentleman was in because he had an infection in his heart and had been rushed down from well north of Grand Rapids to a more qualified hospital. He had originally been treated at a smaller hospital up north, but had to make the trip south due to worsening prognosis.

I am, by nature, a social animal. Within an hour of

his being in my room, I introduced myself through the curtain separating us. We soon got to talking, and within about thirty minutes, we asked a nurse to draw the curtain back so we could talk directly to each other. Over the next several hours we got to know each other, commiserating on the suffering and encouraging each other.

That night, I asked him a question that seemed to come out of nowhere. I asked him if he went to church or believed in God, or some other higher power. He said that he had not been to church in years, but would love to find some place in his area. I asked if I could pray for him, and if I could have my church pray for him. He agreed, and I contacted my church's prayer team, who I knew very well.

The next day, I spent a little more time talking with him before his wife and kids joined him. I was happy to meet her and his boys. A short time later, he was taken away for surgery to clean out the infection in his heart. He never came back up to my room. I found out from his wife that surgical complications meant he was transferred to the Intensive Care Unit (ICU) after surgery. Thankfully, he eventually got rid of the infection. We still maintain contact through social media, and I am glad I was in a position where I could help him in a real dark spot, even when I was in the middle of a dark spot, myself.

Because the infection was rearing its ugly head

again, I once again had to have a PICC line installed for IV antibiotics. This time, they were able to install it in my arm while I was still in my room. A special portable ultrasound and a trained technician meant I did not have to be wheeled down for yet another surgery. My infectious disease doctor prescribed a much higher dose of the same antibiotics that had been working before the last surgery, and I went home for another several weeks of home care.

Molly was assigned to my case for the final time. The first day she came out to the house for the intake paperwork, she set aside extra time to talk with me. Over the course of an hour and a half, we talked about what was coming up. She expressed a very sincere sympathy, and asked me how I was dealing with the upcoming amputation.

I admitted to some of the pain, but I tried to mask as much as possible. Using the dark humor I mentioned previously, I wanted to to laugh as much as possible. So I told jokes. We discussed pirate names and one-legged halloween costumes. *[Side note: Best I've ever seen is an amputee dressing as the lamp from The Christmas Story. He wore fishnets and a lampshade. Freakin' hysterical.]* I'm sure she was perceptive enough to see through my mask, but it was cathartic to laugh with her.

During that time, Chris and I also received a visit from Stephanie at our house. She and her assistant

Nichole came out to the house to talk about the process. They talked about the usual timelines of care, including inpatient stay length, how long it takes to get your first prosthetic limb, and the usual timeline for outpatient therapy. They also brought a leg with them to show as an example. Their visit helped alleviate some of my questions, and a few of my fears.

TREADING WATER

> "Everything can be taken from a man but one thing: the last of the human freedoms — to choose one's attitude in any given set of circumstances, to choose one's own way."
> **Viktor Frankl**

The entire time I was home from the hospital, I was fighting a losing battle with grief and fear. I tried to use humor. I tried to distract myself with friends and family. I even tried to distract myself with writing. All of it helped to some degree, but it was always simply masking over the pain.

I told you I have a dark sense of humor. Some

would say it is rather twisted. I knew that I had to find some way to cope with the grief and loss. I have some amazing friends, some of whom are just as twisted and dark as I am. One of them was Jessie. She came to visit me a lot before my surgery, spending time trying to keep me cheered up. Because she is a security professional dealing with crap from university students, professors, and staff, she shares a good portion of my dark humor.

She also knits. I mention this because one of our conversations became the source for much amusement before, and after, my amputation. We were talking about prosthetic legs and residual limb covers. I talked about getting one that looked like a wooden leg. We started riffing off of each other, and I made a suggestion that I needed a knitted shark as a "stump cover." Jessie knows my fondness for the dark and creepy and we started talking about having tentacles hangin off my limb, as if I was an Lovecraftian horror gone wrong.

As we were talking about the tentacles, I was searching the web and found a hat that was made in the shape of a great white shark, with exaggerated teeth and eyes. I bought it, fully intending to have the shark as a cover. Then Jessie started planning and making a cover that has green tentacles hanging off the end. She finished that one shortly after I was home from the hospital.

Even while distracting myself with dark humor and friends, I also needed something deeper that I could grasp. That had to be hope. I learned to rely on hope which was higher than temporary things or people. I had nothing else to really grasp on to. Things were temporary. People could fail me. I had to have a higher hope. My belief and hope in Christ as a Christian became the life preserver in a sea that was roiling around. Even through the darkest night, I had a hope to which I could cling. It was this hope that I kept clinging to through the last eighteen months. It was this hope that I had to cling to for the future.

About a week before Christmas, I received a call that the surgery had to be postponed. The doctor had a priority pediatric case come up, so we were pushing the surgery back until January 8th, 2019.

That sucked. All of the worry. All of the anticipation. All of the fears. All of them had to wait another two weeks. On the outside, I tried to maintain an even keel. I kept trying to laugh, but I hurt on the inside. A lot.

The one shining moment of that long wait was Christmas Eve service at church. My wife and I have six kids. At the time, we had a minivan that held eight. That worked for our family. Normally. As it was, I had to leave my leg stretched out in a brace, and so I took up an entire row of seats in the van. Due to the special service, we arranged with some friends to help transport some of our kids so that I could sit in the van and go to church.

It was amazing to finally leave the house and go to church with my family. I had only left the house for short trips to doctor appointments or to the one convention. It had been two months since I had walked (rolled) through the front doors of the church, and it was truly a blessing to be able to be back. The warmth in the greetings and prayers were amazing. That evening, Pastor Brian preached a very timely message about grief and anticipation as it related to the birth of Christ and the call to serve him. I felt like the message was what I needed to hear.

Two interminable weeks later, I was driven down to Spectrum Hospital way too early in the morning to be prepped for surgery. I tried to approach it with a good attitude, but I was shaking inside. I had no idea what the future held. My parents had come into town to be with me during the surgery and a few days afterward. My wife was there for me. One of my pastors even came down to pray with me and my family before I went into surgery.

But it all became crystal clear during prep for the surgery. I spent time answering the questions from the nurse, and then talked to the anesthesiologist about the procedure and about my history with anesthesia. Dr. Steensma came in to talk with me before the surgery, and he had me mark the leg that was going to be amputated with a permanent marker. At that moment, I marked my right leg to be removed from my body. He then marked next to my mark to confirm that the right leg would be amputated. It took everything in me at that point to not cry. I had to be brave for my wife and family.

That is a terrible social convention–and a good one at the same time. "Being brave" about an event, a trauma, or other loss is a tradition where the person is considered "brave" when they show little or no sadness, remorse, or grief due to the traumatic event. Where it may be helpful in some circumstances, especially when the witnesses are younger children or those who are not emotionally able to handle the traumatic results, I would bet that there are many cases where "being brave" is actually a cop out, an act to show how strong the person is, to puff up their reputation. I almost wonder if, sometimes, it would be better to not "be brave", and instead acknowledge the trauma. The acknowledgement itself is often part of the Kubler-Ross model of grief, and early action might be more cathartic, and even shortcut the grief.

Maybe. Either way, I was "brave" and went into surgery hiding my fears and grief the best I could.

Then I gave my wife a kiss and was wheeled away to the operating room.

THE NEW NORMAL

I woke up from surgery almost fifty pounds lighter. I do not recommend this type of drastic weight loss surgery, but it does work. In truth, I woke up confused, in pain and afraid to look at my stump. Sorry. The polite term is residual limb. The scariest part of waking up after surgery was trying to move that leg. It felt... odd. Unbalanced. It was far more painful than any time, other than the initial shattering.

But I was alive. The pain. Oh the pain. For the first time in a long time, I gladly accepted narcotics to get the pain under control. When I woke up, my wife, mom, and dad were all present. I do not remember much about that day. I know I was in pain, and I fell back to sleep when that pain was relieved. I remember waking up the next morning.

The next morning, I woke up because of the pain. After the pain meds kicked in, and I had a (very) little bit of breakfast, I was coherent enough to talk to Chris and my parents. When I tried to sit up, I used my legs as counter-weights, as most people do. At least I tried to use my legs. I used one leg and part of the other, wildly shifting me off balance, and scaring me in the process. It was an incredibly vivid reminder that I was forever, irrevocably, changed.

The doctor came in and examined my leg. He unwound all the pressure bandages, and then looked at the dressings that were on the wound itself. This was the first time I would see my new right leg. It was short and swollen. The ugly incision from my last surgery had barely healed over, and that scar now bisected with a scar running across the end of my leg laterally, bisecting the end into upper and lower halves.

I think I was shell-shocked. I did notice that the residual limb was actually longer that it was originally supposed to be. I asked Dr. Steensma about it, and he explained that he had been able to save far more of the femur than he thought he could. He had packed the cored out femur with an antibiotic cement, strengthening the bone, and had then wrapped the muscles around the distal end of the femur.

He told me the incredible swelling was normal for an amputation, and it usually took a long time for the limb to reduce. I was still emotionally numb during the conversation, so I am sure that I missed a fair amount. That information, however, was the important bits. The surgery had taken a long time, but the connections were solid, and I should have a good recovery. I would be in Spectrum for a couple days before being transferred to Mary Free Bed for inpatient care.

I also received a visit from Dr. Simeunovic that morning. She was somber and sympathetic when she visited. She expressed sympathy for my situation, and wished it had gone the other way. We also talked about the upcoming treatments. I was going to be on IV antibiotics for a while, just to finally kill off the MSSA once and for all. Once I was done with that course of antibiotics, I would hopefully, finally be free of the infection.

Later that day, the emotional numbness began to wear off. The grief and loss hit me hard, but I could not, would not, refused to, give in to them. I had support from my family and friends, and I was intending to put on the brave face and laugh through the pain.

I am convinced that part of my personality, part of my energy, and part of my strength actually comes from making people laugh. I get to laugh along with people who are laughing, and that laughing is cathartic and part of my coping mechanism. I had a dark sense of humor, was surrounded by nurses, who also usually have a dark sense of humor, and I had a fake shark.

Eventually, one of my nurses came in to check my vitals and make her rounds. I said to her that I had a really unusual pain in my leg right then and asked her to look at it. I pulled back the sheet and revealed the shark-hat "eating" the end of my stump. She laughed hard, and by the time we were done laughing together, I was worn out and she was wiping tears from her eyes.

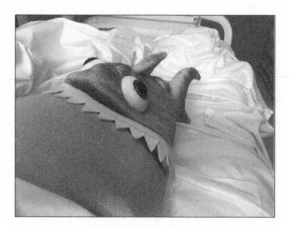

Picked up a Hitchhiker!

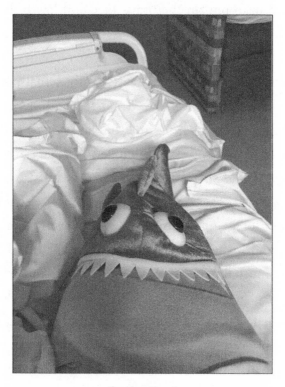

OmNomNom!

I repeated that gag for the next couple nurses who came in the room, as well as any visitors who came to visit me. I got joy out of making people laugh. Dr. Steensma got a, ahem, kick out of it too. By making fun of the situation, I was learning how to chop the problem down to size. [*Yes, those were terrible puns. Get used to it.*]

Laughter really does heal. In the very least, it covers the pain and grief well.

A few days later, I was declared well enough to be transferred to Mary Free Bed. Transferring from the hospital bed to the gurney was an experience itself, and it gave a glimpse into my near future. Muscles and willpower were what it took to slide me from the hospital bed to the gurney.

The cold ambulance ride and transfer to Mary Free Bed was shocking to my system. I was wheeled into a room, and then the hard process of transferring from the gurney to the new bed was even worse. In the end I was exhausted, sore, and wondering what life would be like for the next couple weeks. After the initial flurry of nursing activity, I settled in to watch tv until I fell asleep.

Let me describe one of the rooms in Mary Free Bed. Thankfully, each room was single occupancy. Behind the bed is a mural from a woodland scene. Yes, behind the bed, where the patient cannot see it. The hospital bed takes up the middle of the room. Each room has a row of windows to the outside, and below those windows is a couch that pulls out into a futon. There are some cabinets for storing clothes and other items. A flat-screen tv is mounted on the wall opposite of the bed, with an array of cable and curated movie channels to watch. This tv also shows the patient's daily schedule, as well as important hospital information.

Each room has a very large bathroom with roll-in shower and large toilet area–all big enough to maneuver a wheelchair around. The sink is high enough to pull a chair up underneath. The door to the bathroom is a sliding barn-style door, which allows for full use of all the space, without worries about getting trapped behind doors.

Mary Free Bed is a full hospital, and is fully staffed with some of the best nurses and aides around. Each floor has access to several different therapy gyms, as well as a couple different patient lounges. These lounges have vending machines, but also hold seating areas and tables where friends and family of the patients can gather outside the room. Patients can also wander down to the lounges and hang out, enjoying larger windows and places to comfortably gather socially.

In short, I was in a place that I knew well, and I was ready to start my road to recovery. Whatever that turned out to be.

DRY DOCK

“ The friend who can be silent with us in a
moment of despair or confusion, who can
stay with us in an hour of grief and
bereavement, who can tolerate not
knowing... not healing, not curing... that is
a friend who cares.

Henri Nouwen

~

The first full day at Mary Free Bed started
rough. At 6:45am I met my new doctor for
the first time. Dr. Bruinsma is the Medical Director of
the orthotics and amputee programs at the hospital,
and he was now my doctor. I have never been a
morning person, and 6:45am was way too early for

me. I struggled to become coherent enough to talk to Dr. Bruinsma, and eventually was able to talk to him about the program and prognosis. He examined the wound, and we talked about the goals and approximate times of my inpatient stay. Then he continued his rounds.

Breakfast was soon brought in, and I remembered how bad the hospital food was. I was also in pain, and really did not want to start with physical therapy. I was not feeling well. But I was determined to push through. Somewhere in the past couple days I had decided that I would not let the grief and loss take hold any more than they already had.

Remember, I had been here at this hospital four times before as an inpatient client. Being in that bed, in that hospital, made me remember some of the lessons that I had learned ten years prior. I remembered vividly that my attitude, my willingness to work, was what would set the stage for my recovery. I also knew, beyond a shadow of a doubt, that I would eventually be better off with this amputation.

Oh, I still hurt. I still grieved. But I stubbornly refused to allow that to determine who I was going to be. I refused to let the grief define me. I somehow knew that I needed to start to define myself. As a layperson, I knew the basic thoughts about the Kubler-Ross Stages of Grief, and I knew, in my soul, that I had to accept the loss.

Gritting my teeth through the pain, I ate a little bit of breakfast. The nurse brought me my morning meds, including the pain meds, and then I had her hand me the shark-hat. I knew that my new Occupational Therapist would be coming in to help me get ready for the day, and I wanted to start with a laugh. I was determined to make all of my primary therapists laugh that first day. So I put the shark on the end of my stump and covered it with a sheet.

When my OT arrived, I was awake and watching some morning television program. Turning off the tv, I greeted her and we exchanged names and pleasantries. Monica smiled and asked if I was ready to get out of bed that day. I nodded and pulled the sheet off my lower body. There it was. A comical shark appeared to be chewing on my stump. We both laughed, and then I realized that I now had to get up and out of my bed.

This was one of the first times that I was going to get out of my bed, and she was there to help me get ready. She was also there to help me figure out how to transfer from the bed to the wheelchair, and from the wheelchair to the toilet, and vice versa. As I said before, sitting up was a struggle, getting your balance without using, in my case, fifty pounds of counterweight was rough. I started out that session smiling. I ended that session exhausted and frustrated.

As we were ending that session, I stayed in my

wheelchair. Within a few days, this would become my habit. Once I was out of bed for the day, it was rare that I was back in bed until after all of my therapies for the day. Even then, it was usually almost bed time before I decided to lay back in my bed.

As Monica was getting ready to leave, my new Physical Therapist was entering the room. Greg and I introduced ourselves to each other, and we chatted as we began to wheel out of the room and down to one of the therapy gyms. By the time I had rolled about forty or fifty feet, I was exhausted. Greg took over, and pushed my chair down the hallway to the gym. We talked about my background, and eventually arrived at the therapy gym.

At Mary Free Bed, the therapy gyms are often crammed with exercise equipment designed to allow anyone, with almost any ailment or loss, to build their strength. There were also sets of parallel bars and low-slung therapy beds where patients could stretch comfortably on mats, while off the floor. That morning, we began a routine of stretching, strength exercises, and practicing balancing. We also worked on walking/hopping with the walker to make sure that I was safe. By the time we were done for that session, I was completely wrung out. I mopped my face and neck with a towel as Greg pushed me back to my room for lunch.

After lunch, I had another OT session and another

PT session. For occupational therapy, we went and played a couple board games. Why? Because part of OT is designed to make sure that the mental faculties and social skills of the patient were as well maintained, and improved as fast as, the physical skills. I rather enjoyed my afternoon OT sessions, as I love to play board and card games. Talking about other games while I played with Monica and the occasional intern really helped keep my spirits buoyed.

For my afternoon physical therapy session, we went to a different therapy gym. There I concentrated on building my arm strength and endurance using a hand bike and the parallel bars. By three o'clock, I was done. Exhausted, I wanted nothing more than to somehow crawl up into my bed and sleep.

Why the extreme workout? Mary Free Bed's philosophy is to assign a specific number of hours of therapy to the patient per week. This is determined by their therapy goals and their general health. If the patient accomplished all of their sessions during the week, they might have one session on Saturday, and have Sunday off. Skip a day or two of therapy? You were working on therapy all weekend.

This seemed cruel at times, but I understand why they do it that way. This rigorous schedule allows the patient to recover physically and mentally in the best time frame, while keeping them busy enough to help them get past any grief or loss.

That night, my wife brought the rest of my kids to the hospital to see me. They had not seen me since the surgery, and it was four days later. My heart broke as my almost-six-year-old hid behind Chris and my almost-ten-year-old shrank back. Neither one of them recognized me. I was not well groomed. Where I am normally clean shaven, I was sporting a five-day growth of beard, and it had grown in mostly silver and white. Instead of my contacts, I was wearing my glasses. In short, I was a stranger.

After the other kids hugged me and talked to me, Brie, my almost-ten-year-old, came to hug me. This was my little girl, the one I had held when she was an infant and I was recovering from my original surgery, and she was scared of me. Eventually, my littlest one came to hug me, just before the family had to leave. That night after they left I was hurting very badly, and went to sleep with an ache in my soul.

Most of the days in the hospital were better than that one. Most of them. I tried my best to maintain a positive attitude, and really tried to smile and laugh when I had visitors. I tried to smile and laugh with my nurses and aides. I also tried to smile and laugh with my therapists.

SNIPPETS OF MEMORIES

A couple days after I arrived at Mary Free Bed, I was hungry for some real food. My friend David and his wife decided to visit with me, and he asked what I wanted for dinner. I was craving good Thai food, and one of the best Thai restaurants in the city was only a couple blocks from the hospital. I asked for Curry Pad Thai, and he and his wife brought Thai food for all three of us to the hospital. We rolled down to one of the passenger lounges, and I really enjoyed the food that night. I know it smelled great, because we had about a half dozen nurses stop us as we were walking to ask what we had and where we got it.

My wife, Chris, spent several mornings with me. She would show up before Monica arrived, and I would be dressed for the day by my OT session time. I cherished those mornings, hearing from her about what was going on at home.

Brent and Nichole came up to my room one night after they were done with work and visited with me. They both were very supportive and wanted to help cheer me up. We had worked together, on and off, for almost five years, and I truly believe both of them are some of the best physical therapists out there. It was a bittersweet visit. I knew that my next outpatient phys-ical therapy would have to be with someone who specialized in amputations, so I would never work with them again. However, I was able to show off the huge hunk of cobalt-chromium that had been my knee for so long. They were both amazed that the contraption had been my knee for nearly ten years.

I had a couple rough days where grief and loss overwhelmed me. One of those days I ended up not doing any therapy all day. I begged off from both OT and PT. I just needed time to cope with the sudden onset of emotions. That day ended with tears.

My youngest celebrated her sixth birthday in Mary Free Bed with me. Chris brought a cake, presents, and a game to play with the kids while we celebrated the little one's birthday. My smile was a mask for the pain when I realized that I was missing my kids lives while I was in the hospital.

My regular gaming group joined me for a night of boardgames. They brought food, snacks, and the games on what would have been our normal Friday night. The night of games and laughter was an amazing buoy for my spirits.

I remember being taken to a doctor's appointment in a wheelchair via medical transport. This was a followup appointment with Dr. Steensma and his PA, Stacy. It was mid January in Michigan, and the windchill was almost subzero. I had a pair of sweats, a t-shirt, and a light jacket for that cold trip. My biggest regret that trip? Not bringing my wallet. The ambulance driver was willing to run through a drive-thru at a fast food restaurant, but I had forgotten my wallet in my room.

A couple of my friends became regular visitors during my stay. David visited me often, coming up after work and playing games or just chatting while I recovered from the day's therapy. Jessie also visited regularly. Her work was just a few blocks away from the hospital, so she would often stop by to keep me company when Chris could not be there due to taking care of the kids.

A couple of my pastors were also regular visitors. As one of the safety team leaders, my direct boss, Pastor David, came to visit me often. He knew how much I was suffering while not attending and serving at the church, and he made sure to become a regular. Pastor Jim, who was in charge of Pastoral Care, was also a frequent visitor. Their visits and prayers always lifted my spirits.

DEALING WITH PHANTOM PAIN

While I was in the hospital for inpatient therapy, I began to deal with phantom sensations and phantom pain. For those who might not know, most amputees will have phantom sensations and/or phantom pain at some point after their surgery. What is the difference? Phantom sensation is the sensation that the body can still feel and communicate with the missing limb. The patient knows where the limb "is" and even has a sense of which direction it is pointing. Phantom pain is a psychosomatic sensation that the missing limb is in pain or in distress.

I began dealing with phantom pain and phantom sensation just a couple days after I arrived at Mary Free Bed. When I was not in pain, I "knew" exactly where my lower leg was. When I was in bed, I could feel it pointing straight down through the mattress at a ninety degree angle. When I was sitting in my wheelchair, it again hung down at a ninety degree angle, right where it should. Standing up at the parallel bars? The leg was straight down, and I could almost feel the ground beneath it.

The irony did not escape me that I could now bend a knee that was not actually there farther than I could when I still had the knee. I could also move the muscles in my leg and feel my lower leg swing back and forth like a pendulum. I could swing it front-to-back and even side-to-side. I can now swing the lower leg in a complete three-sixty going through all the points in a compass. I should not have to tell you that being able to feel and move a leg that was not there was more than a bit distracting, especially at night.

What about the phantom pain? It sucks. I am not a doctor, but I understand that the nerves that run down into the limbs are connected into very specific areas of the brain. Nerves are designed to be early warning indicators of danger and distress for the extremities. A burn will cause a specific signal, and the brain interprets that into pain, causing voluntary and involuntary reactions. So what. Those nerves are gone right? No signals getting through is good, right?

Wrong. The complete lack of signal is another indicator for the human brain that something is wrong on that limb. This occasionally will generate a "pain" signal and the brain informs the rest of the body that the limb is in danger. Phantom pain cannot be dealt with by physical means. And sometimes that pain gets great enough that something needs to be done.

I began to develop phantom pains, especially late at night. When the attacks came on, the only way to get rid of the psychosomatic pain signals was to treat the signals with real, physical narcotics. It became a vicious cycle, and one that I dreaded. That was when Dr. Bruinsma prescribed a low dose of a neural-blocker/anti-convulsant called Gabapentin. Also used for seizures, this medicine blocks certain low-level neural activity, and has been shown to help with false or "phantom" pains. It usually helped.

The worse phantom pain I ever suffered was a muscle cramp in the back of the calf that was not there. When a muscle cramps and hurts, the pain can usually be mitigated by rubbing and slowly working the muscle until those fibers stop firing convulsively.

This usually does not take too long, and is rarely serious. When the same cramp happened in my right calf, the one that was not there, I could not do anything about it except wait for the pain to go away. For two hours my "calf" suffered a paralyzing cramp, and there was nothing I could do except cry. The Gabapentin and pain meds helped in that one area. Unfortunately, they hurt me in a very important area.

I am an author and artist. I am, by definition, a creative professional, and I was on a medicine that blocked neurons from firing in my brain. Dr. Bruinsma prescribed a very low dosage of the Gabapentin, and he warned me about the possible side effects, but I was desperate for any kind of relief. So I began taking the meds, and within a few days I could tell that something was wrong.

I was thinking slower. I could not concentrate. I could not write anything. I was becoming forgetful. The worst part of the equation was that I could not equate the slower thinking and less creativity to the meds. Originally, I knew it was a potential side effect, but I was on such a low dose that it should not have been affecting me. Besides, the meds were helping with the crazy phantom pains, and I needed that relief.

So what did I do? I struggled on. I fought forward with sheer willpower. Remember, it is hard for me to ask for help, to acknowledge something is broken in my life. I had lived with pain for years, so this could be overcome as well. *[Side Note: Please do not take this as advice to not take or to stop taking this type of medication. It affects everyone differently, and I know several people that take higher doses of Gabapentin and function flawlessly. Every person is different and every situation is different. Work with your doctor to alleviate the phantom pain.]*

Through it all, I maintained my hope. I could laugh because I knew what was finite and what was infinite. Even while feeling slower than normal, I knew where my hope lay, and I tried to derive joy from life around me.

SETTING SAIL

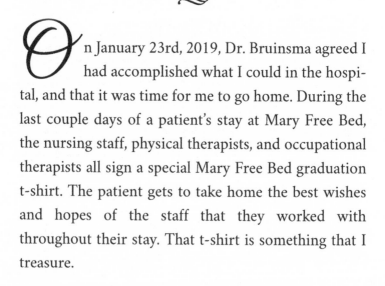

> My hope still is to leave the world a bit
> better than when I got here.
> **Jim Henson**

On January 23rd, 2019, Dr. Bruinsma agreed I had accomplished what I could in the hospital, and that it was time for me to go home. During the last couple days of a patient's stay at Mary Free Bed, the nursing staff, physical therapists, and occupational therapists all sign a special Mary Free Bed graduation t-shirt. The patient gets to take home the best wishes and hopes of the staff that they worked with throughout their stay. That t-shirt is something that I treasure.

That cold January day, my wife loaded me into the minivan and we went home. I rolled up the ramp into our house, missing most of my leg and being very glad to be home. Our cat, Zoe, greeted me at the door, and jumped up on my lap. She stayed there for hours, making sure I would not leave again. I had left her for over two weeks. This was an eternity to the kitten, and she would never let me forget it. Having her on my lap was one of the best parts about coming home that day.

The next couple weeks were filled with hectic activity as I tried to adjust to my new normal. Struggles with doorways and furniture arrangements compounded with the finishing touches and prepping my new office upended any semblance of routine. In and amongst the chaos, I was tryin desperately to finish a project that I had been working on for over twenty years. I was determined to finish and publish my first roleplaying game.

Working on the game and the related book, I noticed that I would often struggle to find the right word in my vocabulary. I also was far more scatter-brained and forgetful than I was before the surgery. This was maddening, until I was able to guess that the Gabapentin and narcotic pain medications were physically interfering with my neural signals, which meant I was less creative and more scattered. It was a weird sensation to want to write, to want to tell a story, and yet feel as if I was pulling the story out of a bowl of wet noodles , unable to grasp more than a little at a time. I could feel the story slip away when I tried to grab it, and grew frustrated. I lived with this fogginess for a couple months, until I was able to wean off the Gabapentin. Unfortunately, I still occasionally suffer from the lingering effects.

As I was recovering at home and starting to get back to work, I was waiting for the giant incision across the end of my residual limb to heal fully. Only then could I begin the process to get a prosthetic. The process goes through several stages, and I was impatient to work through mine.

For a new amputee, the patient can begin to use a wrap called a "shrinker" once the wound from the amputation heals. The shrinker is a sleeve that fits over the end of the residual limb to start squeezing the swelling and fluids out of the stump. This is necessary before an amputee can even begin to be fitted for their first prosthetic.

When a limb is amputated, the fluids that would normally move throughout the limb have no where to go. Add to that the long inactivity, and the residual limb, the leftover stump, begins to swell. This is normal for amputation patients. The cloth shrinker begins the process of applying compression to help push those fluids out of the limb. Like most compression-style aids, the patient has to start with spending small amounts of time in the shrinker, gradually increasing their time until it is worn for the vast majority of the day.

A short time after I went home, Stephanie came out to my house from Mary Free Bed to bring me my first shrinker. It is basically a compression sleeve that is attached to a velcro belt, securing the shrinker to the patient's body. I welcomed the shrinker, as it was the first step to getting my prosthetic.

After about a month, the shrinker had made huge improvements, and I was ready for fitting a prosthetic. I was introduced to Alisha, my prosthetist. *[Side Note: Be careful when pronouncing this title. It is not hard for the sentence, "I'm going to see Alisha, my prosthetist" to be mumbled in a way to change the meaning drastically.]* There are many different ways to test fit and create a mold for a prosthetic socket.

For this first socket, Alisha took many measurements of my leg, at specific intervals, measuring the circumference, the height to various key locations, and also the length. She created a rendering in a CAD software, and created a mold from that. This turned into a plastic socket that could be tested and adjusted with a heat gun. Once she was satisfied, she made my first socket, attaching a hydraulic knee assembly and foot. Then it was time for physical therapy. It was time to learn how to walk.

One of the coolest things about the socket design used at Mary Free Bed, is that the final layer of the socket creation embeds the cloth pattern of your choice to decorate your new socket. I am a graphic designer and artist by trade, and have amazing connections in the printing industry. This allowed me to have a very cool image of a dragon on a very colorful background laminated into the socket. Alisha told me she showed off the prosthetic to several people before it was finally delivered to me.

As I got my prosthetic leg, I could see some hope, some light at the end of the tunnel. My spirits were lifted higher, and it looked like the worst of it was over. For the most part, that was true. I was generally in much higher spirits. I was trying to put the grief and loss behind me, and it usually worked. Usually.

Do not get the impression that all my down times were gone, and that everything was "coming up roses" with the amputation. I still had dark days. There were times when the pain and hurt was back, and the frustration made it impossible to smile. I have never knowingly drank alcohol, nor have I ever imbibed recreational narcotics. But I fully understand why some folks do drink or do drugs. I remember thinking several times that I wouldn't mind the effects of having a couple good stiff shots of liquor just to take the pain and cares away for a little bit.

I was fortunate. I still am fortunate. When I hit that low point, actually contemplating drowning my sorrows in alcohol or drugs, I instead know that I have a higher hope, a higher peace to embrace. It is tough. The temptation is there, and the excuses could easily be used to numb the pain. I do not fault anyone who feels like they are driven to that point. I just know there is a better way.

One of the most amazing statements I heard once I was able to start attending church again after the amputation was from a dear friend. Sandie had known me for years, and had watched me struggle with pain while serving. She told me that this was the first time she had seen me without pain, ever. She said it was like a visible weight had lifted from my shoulders, and that I seemed genuinely happier. Once I thought about it, I had to agree with her. It was the first time in ten long years that I did not feel pain in my right knee. That burden was finally gone.

That can sometimes happen. When we have lived with a chronic condition, such as pain, for a long time, the sudden relief of that condition will feel like a weight has lifted. That burden is no longer strapped across our back. And that was an amazing experience to recognize.

LESSONS FROM PT

Once I received my prosthetic, I had to learn how to walk. I was impatient. I was eager. I was often ahead of expectations when working with physical therapy, and

I was waiting for that to happen again. I wanted to run. Then reality dropped on me.

I had an Above Knee amputation–an AK in medical terms. I figured that I would fit the prosthetic leg and be able to stand and walk very soon. No. In physical therapy, I was introduced to Sarah and Kristen. They would become my new torturers–er... physical therapists. Sarah was my lead PT; she got me started and helped me work with other therapies to reduce phantom pain. Kristen took over from Sarah when Sarah's schedule conflicted with mine, teaching me to walk and practicing with me.

Learning to walk was difficult. I had been walking since I was a toddler, and was used to the typical unconscious movement of walking. My muscles knew how to walk, and they did. Now, all of those muscles were gone or severely limited, and brand new muscles were needed to walk, understanding that there is no feedback below the knee.

What is that like? Think about sitting in such a way that one of your legs falls asleep. Make sure it is good an numb. No sensation in that foot and calf? Great. Now stand up and walk. Do not hesitate. Stand up right now and take a couple steps. If you did not fall, you are lucky. You probably had to stand there waiting to get some feeling back in your foot so that you could feel the floor beneath you. Before those pins and needles of the blood returning to your leg kick in, that numbness is *almost* how little I feel. I have no feeling, no sensation below the knee, unless it is a phantom sensation.

So I had to learn to walk on a leg that had no sensation, no feeling. How do you walk with the prosthetic? Think of paddling a canoe. You lean forward and dig that paddle into the water. Using both arms, you drag that paddle back toward you using your shoulder and back muscles, sliding the canoe through the water. Congratulations. That is how you walk with a prosthetic.

Plant the heel of the prosthetic. Use your hip and glutes to drag that leg backward, all while making sure to keep enough pressure back on the leg to lock the knee. Make sure you have that knee locked, or your knee will go limp and bend, and you will fall. On ice or snow? Short steps, keeping the knee stiff. Rough terrain? The same. Your leg muscles are constantly firing to make sure that prosthetic knee is locked.

Even standing still requires effort and concentration. Let that hydraulic knee unlock, and the rapid release mechanism will make your knee buckle so fast, you will be on the ground before you know why. Studies show that walking with an AK and prosthetic requires almost 300% more energy that a normal human adult walking. That AK amputee basically walks three times as far as you do to travel the same distance.

I would love to tell you that I stood up and walked in just a day or two. That would be the fairy tale ending of this story. In reality, I learned to take really small steps in the parallel bars. When I kind of learned to do that, we graduated to a walker, making short laps around the outpatient therapy gym. More precisely, I would make a short lap and get tired and have to sit down. Then I told Kristen that I wanted to learn to use forearm crutches.

The next time I was in for therapy, she strapped me into a harness and hooked me up to a track system built into the ceiling. This system was designed to allow me to walk with very light support from the harness. When I fell, the harness would catch me and the emergency braking system would stop my fall within a few inches of starting to fall. I was loaned a pair of crutches and prepared to take my first step. I fell.

By the end of that day, I could take a couple steps, synchronizing the forearm crutches and using them as almost regular crutches. I was also physically wrecked and exhausted. Within a few more sessions, I was walking the entire length of the overhead track, about 130 feet, without falling. I had even learned how to turn around. I felt like I was ready to walk without the harness. The hard work was starting to pay off.

Back into the therapy gym, and I was learning more and more to walk with the forearm crutches.

Once I was able to walk on indoor floor surfaces, I had to learn to walk over uneven surfaces, up and down ramps and stairs, and even how to pick things up while standing (that's a lot harder than it looks). I had goals, and I was working toward a new normal life. I had hope.

I worked hard. I often hurt after physical therapy. But I got better. Then I noticed some physical changes to my residual limb. When an amputee starts to work that limb, certain muscles that had been prominent before would no longer be used, and would wither away. Other muscles that had never been used were now getting their workout, which means they grow, replacing the weakened and withering ones.

My leg shrank in circumference and length. The muscle tone also changed with the new muscle shapes. In short, the shape of my leg changed drastically. This is fully expected throughout the first year or two. In just a few months my socket was loose enough that it was causing me a great deal of instability and frustration. I had just learned to walk, and was unable to continue physical therapy because I was actually losing ground due to the instability. This meant it was time for a new socket.

I stopped attending PT while I waited for my new socket to be built. This particular socket was going to be a dragon skin pattern with a tear in the skin and glowing cybernetics shining through. And while I impatiently waited for my socket, I was offered a chance to have recreational therapy. This meant that I was able to be trained to get in and out of the therapy pool at the hospital, and was able to re-learn how to swim. The first time I tried a freestyle kick I flailed ineffectually. It was terrifying and weird at the same time.

Once I got my second socket, I was back with Kristen in PT. One of the most terrifying, and yet free-ing, experiences, was learning how to fall. Someone who has an AK amputation will eventually fall. A momentary inattentiveness and a backward step caused my first fall after the surgery. This was terrify-ing, because once I start to fall, there is nothing stop-ping me. No muscles. I am about six and a half feet tall, so I have a long ways to fall. Fortunately, I had learned how to fall, and therefore had learned how to get back up.

If we are going to fall, we probably should figure out how to fall well, and then figure out how to get up again. Because that is the second part to the falling lesson–getting back up. Kristen taught me how to fall, and then helped me figure out how to get back up without anyone else around. Having someone help you stand up again is a risky proposition. If they pull the wrong way, or do not help enough, their good intentions are not enough to keep from crashing back down to the ground again. On the flip side, if they know how to help you, they will make getting up easier, and safer. It seems like there is a life lesson there.

Physical therapy for me was an awful lot like life in general, and I was able to learn some life lessons from it. I do not want to trivialize my experience, but if I had to sum it up, I would probably do so like this:

- When catastrophe strikes and cuts the legs right out from underneath us, we need to figure out how to re-learn to walk again. It may be slow and painful, but the payoff in the end is the new normal.
- Sometimes we are off kilter while trying to swim through life. When disaster strikes, we can easily flail around ineffectually. Again, we have to re-learn how to balance and move in the conditions after the disaster.
- We have to learn how to fall. We will fall at some point in life. Only after we learn how to fall can we learn how to get back up. And we must choose really carefully who we ask for help.

Eventually, I reached a point in my therapy where any gains that I made were very minor. Kristen recommended that we stop therapy, and I agreed. At that point, it was a matter of gradually getting better at walking, and better getting used to my new normal.

You have heard that phrase many times here–the "new normal." This outlook, this philosophy, is the summation of hope. It is the acceptance that the stuff in the past is just that, in the past. The infection and complications are in the past. I have to move forward. To look forward, I have to accept that the conditions that I am left with are going to be my new normal. Accepting what has happened helps get me through the grief and loss, and that acceptance allows me to have hope in the future. That is my new normal.

CATCHING THE WIND

> Regardless of whatever I do, I know what my purpose is: to make a difference in people's lives.
>
> **Tim Tebow**

~

Since my amputation, I have become a mentor to new amputees at Mary Free Bed. What do I do as a mentor? I meet with folks who need to talk to someone about what their new normal is going to be like. For new amputees who are feeling overwhelmed, I walk into their room on my own prosthetic. That is proof that they can move on. I then spend time listening to their fears, answering their questions, and reassuring them that they can find an even keel in their new normal. When they ask, I recount my story. I talk about my struggles. I talk about my low points. I also talk about some of the good things that have happened.

But mostly I tell them that it is ok to cry. I often cannot stress enough that it is ok to grieve. As a new amputee, or as someone who will be having an amputation, it is absolutely good to grieve. As someone who has experienced ANY normal-shattering loss, it is worthwhile to grieve. Grief and feelings of loss are not only normal, they need to be expressed. This is especially true if the amputation is the result of an accident or other emergency. Sure, I am there to provide a few answers, but my main goal, my main "job," is to listen to their fears and grief and then provide some comfort.

Why do I mentor others? Every time I meet with a patient for a mentoring appointment, I am emotionally drained from the encounter. Between dredging up my own experiences, and helping comfort and care for their situation, I become weary. If possible, I use gentle humor to help the patient see their new normal in another light. So why do I do it? Because I have been blessed with a purpose, in some ways a calling, to help provide that comfort and hope to those patients. It is the same reason I wrote this book.

GRIEF AND MEANING

There are a lot of theories that try to break down people's response to grief into various stages, one of which I mentioned earlier is the Kubler-Ross Stages of Grief theory. All of them seem to have some similarities, and all of them really try to encapsulate a process that changes for everyone who experiences grief. In fact the original Kubler-Ross stages was only designed to describe the stages that a terminally ill person actually goes through, not the loved ones and survivors. And it was never designed to describe a linear progression, but a simple description of the various effects of grief on the terminally ill patient.

Why do I bring this up? I already told you I am not a clinical psychologist or doctor. I'm a survivor. That is my bona fides. I worked through the grief and loss of my leg through amputation. This is my experience.

How do I see the recovery from grief and loss? I think there's some truth to the Kubler-Ross model, and its derivatives. If I had to sum it up, for me, my grief recovery happened like this:

- **Shock and Anger:** The first response for me was shock and numbness that I was going to lose my leg. After countless months struggling to keep it, the war was over and I had lost. That made me angry. I was angry at

the situation. I was angry at my doctors.
And I was even angry at God for allowing it.

- **Frustration and Fear:** After I got over the
  heat of my anger, I became frustrated. I
  asked, "Why did this happen to me?"
  Questions about alternative methods and
  wondering if I had done everything I
  possibly could turned to frustration at
  having no substantive answers. Then the
  fear hit. What would life be like after the
  amputation. Would I be able to play with my
  kids. Would I be able to have a normal life? I
  was afraid of the future. I was afraid FOR
  the future.

- **Acceptance and Recovery**: Eventually, I
  was able to accept what would be my new
  normal. I had to "Flip the Switch." I
  consciously made a decision that I was done
  grieving, and had to accept the new normal.
  I had to move forward. That led to
  recovering the pieces of my life. Working
  through the process to figure out what the
  new normal would be, and how to achieve
  that new normal. It was the recovery
  process that would lead me to my final
  stages.

- **Hope and Purpose**: I had to find the hope
  that would guide me through my new

normal. As I have mentioned many times, hope is incredibly important, and I believe that finding hope leads to finding purpose. A life without hope is a life without meaning, without purpose. When I considered my hope, and the source of my hope, I was able to look at my new normal and find purpose.

I have to stress that this is MY interpretation. This is my experience. Again, I am not a clinician or trained therapist. I cannot tell you how you will experience grief and recovery. I can only offer you my experience and hope that it helps.

FLIPPING THE SWITCH

What does "Flip the Switch" mean? When I talk about flipping the switch, I am talking about the moment that I made the conscious decision to not grieve anymore. I was tired of the tears. I was tired of the hurt and pain. And I had worked hard through the anger, frustration , and fear. I accepted that my life would have a new normal, and that I would accept that new normal, making it mine to define. I flipped the switch to turn OFF the tears and to turn ON joy and hope.

I used this term in a recent conversation, and a

friend asked if I knew when my "Flip the Switch" moment was. As I looked at her, she explained that she used the term to explain the moment that she decided to no longer grieve and cry for her recent divorce. She also told me that her other friends who had gone through recent loss or trauma used the same term to describe when they had stopped grieving and accepted the new normal.

If you have not guessed by now, my "Flip the Switch" moment was that day long ago in Spectrum Hospital where I decided that I was tired of crying and tired of grieving. I decided that I needed to laugh, and therefore asked for jokes to fill my social media feed. That was when Jannell asked if it was too early for pirate jokes. That was me flipping the switch.

You may not know the precise moment of your flipping the switch. If you have been through grief and loss, you may have just gradually turned up the lights. But I'm willing to bet that once you have moved beyond your grief, once you have found your hope, you could look back and find the moment you flipped the switch and accepted hope.

FINDING HOPE

So why do I have hope after all the terrible things that have happened to me? Because I can look through the pain, through the grief, and through the loss, and realize that my hope, my help, my burden was borne by someone else. Someone infinite. You may see a long string of medical issues that culminated in an amputation and say, "Where was God? He let you suffer."

I would answer, "He let me choose to respond. He let me choose to grow. And when I relied on His hope, he carried me."

When I start talking about having hope, there are two areas where we can find hope: the finite and the infinite. When we have hope in the finite, it might carry us through temporarily. Finite hope is when we place our hope or consider our hope in the temporary, finite, fallible world. We might have our hope in the machines that help us, or the work and knowledge of the doctors that we see, or even our own bodies. We can also place our finite hope in our friends, family, church, or other organization. Sometimes we even place our hope in the government or insurance company.

It is ok to place some hope in the finite and fallible. As long as your only hope is not in the finite. The problem with hope in the finite world is the fallibility of the finite world. Machines occasionally break. Doctors can sometimes be wrong. Our friends and family can sometimes let us down. And governments and insurance companies look out for themselves, sometimes failing to help us.

When the finite world fails us, our hope can be

shattered, and may re-dredge the grief and muck up from the past. When our hope is shattered, our faith can shatter as well. Whether the faith is in the finite or the infinite, shattered faith can cripple us emotionally and spiritually.

Infinite hope is when we place our hope in some higher power. Whether you believe in God, YHWH, Allah, Gaia, or some other higher power, the hope of the infinite is beyond the fallibility of this world. Infinite hope rises above the fallibility of the world and allows us to look up and forward.

If we have hope in the infinite, the fallible world will not crush our hope. When we look up to the infinite for our hope, we understand that this world is finite and fallible, but that the infinite pulls our hope through.

Having hope requires us to be vulnerable. We have to open up and acknowledge that there is something greater than us. Whether it is finite or infinite, acknowledging that there is something that we need to cling to is ultimately acknowledging that we are insufficient and asking for help. And that asking leaves us vulnerable to potential judgement from others.

Hope in the finite leaves us less vulnerable. Hope in a fallible object means that the object cannot judge our reliance on them. Hoping that a prosthetic leg will make my life better means that the leg cannot judge me for being weak and vulnerable. Hope in a person or community is a bit worse, because that hope leaves us vulnerable to the judgment from the person we have our hope in.

Hope in the infinite is more open, and at the same time, way more vulnerable. Here we risk judgement from the higher power we are desperate to hope on. Critical judgement from the infinite means far more to someone who has hope in the infinite. This takes a tremendous amount of courage to face that potential judgement of our vulnerabilities.

Where is my hope? I have a hope in the infinite. I find great comfort and great hope as a follower of Jesus Christ. When my fallible world causes pain, my infinite hope in Christ is a beacon that I can find. That beacon stands tall and strong, like a lighthouse warning of danger and pointing to the safety of the open water–a rather appropriate metaphor for our talk of ships and pirates.

Our hope, or lack thereof, provides a certain perspective. Hope in life offers a perspective that there might be meaning or purpose in life. If we have hope in something, we can see a purpose to our lives. Conversely, without hope, we are hard put to find meaning or purpose in our lives. When life has no meaning, OUR life has no meaning.

C.S. Lewis wrote about perspective in the book, *The Great Divorce*. In this passage, the two characters are discussing hope and the perception of the infinite. The main character describes the perception.

> That is what mortals misunderstand. They say of some temporal suffering, 'No future bliss can make up for it,' not knowing that Heaven, once attained, will work backwards and turn even that agony into a glory. And of some sinful pleasure they say 'Let me have but this and I'll take the consequences': little dreaming how damnation will spread back and back into their past and contaminate the pleasure of sin. Both processes begin even before death. The good man's past begins to change so that his forgiven sins and remembered sorrows take on the quality of Heaven: the bad man's past already conforms to his badness and is filled only with dreariness. And that is why, at the end of all things, when the sun rises here and the twilight turns to blackness down there, the Blessed will say 'We have never lived anywhere except Heaven,' and the Lost, 'We were always in Hell.' And both will speak truly.
>
> **C.S. Lewis - *The Great Divorce***

Our perspective, our hope, filters the world around us. People without hope, without joy, will always see the worst in this world. They will say, "Things have always been bad. There is no meaning in life." And they are correct–from their own perspective.

Possessing the hope of the infinite affords you the perspective on the important things in this life. With hope, you can say, "Things have always worked toward the good. There is meaning in life." And you will be right. Hope will change your perspective.

It certainly did mine.

FINDING JOY

Once you find hope, you can unlock joy. Real joy is based on hope, and is tinted and enhanced by traveling through and overcoming grief, loss, and suffering. Joy is not mere happiness. Happiness is a fleeting emotion that is based on circumstances of the moment. Joy is a deep knowledge and satisfaction that is based on hope in life.

Joy allows us to laugh heartily and deeply. It is based on understanding that the current situation is in proper perspective. Joy allows us to laugh at ourselves, and to find the humor in our life and situation. Joy allows me to crack pirate and other amputee jokes all the time. My joy allows me to accept the good-natured ribbing from my friends, laughing and responding in kind. My joy gave me the perspective to call my publishing company **Stumped Publishing**.

Helen Keller was no stranger to literal darkness and hardship. Blind and deaf from an illness since the age of nineteen months. She often wrote about joy and happiness.

> The marvelous richness of human experience would lose something of rewarding joy if there were no limitations to overcome. The hilltop hour would not be half so wonderful if there were no dark valleys to traverse.
>
> **Helen Keller – *Light in My Darkness***

I believe that we can only really see the highest mountain peak when we have traveled through the valley. Our joy comes from surviving the loss and grief and finding hope. Our hope then leads us out of the valley, in spite of the darkness. We can then experience the joy of life through hope.

FINDING PURPOSE

When you have hope, either in the finite or the infinite, you can find meaning and purpose in your life. Without hope, there can be no meaning or purpose. Hope is one of the necessary ingredients of Purpose.

How do I define purpose? Purpose is a calling to make the world around you better. That purpose can be as small as making some aspect of yourself better, or as grandiose as trying to save the world. Even changing something about yourself can, and will, change the world directly around you. Finding your purpose requires examining yourself and figuring out what you are called to do. Unfortunately, getting to hope and purpose requires suffering.

Viktor Frankl was a holocaust survivor and psychologist who wrote the book *Man's Search for Meaning*. In the book, Frankl talks about finding meaning in life. To find meaning in life, Frankl believes the person must find meaning in suffering. Read the excerpt below:

> If there is a meaning in life at all, then there must be a meaning in suffering. Suffering is an ineradicable part of life, even as fate and death. Without suffering and death human life cannot be complete.
>
> The way in which a man accepts his fate and all the suffering it entails, the way in which he takes up his cross, gives him ample opportunity — even under the most difficult circumstances — to add a deeper meaning to his life. It may remain brave, dignified and unselfish. Or in the bitter

fight for self-preservation he may forget his human dignity and become no more than an animal. Here lies the chance for a man either to make use of or to forgo the opportunities of attaining the moral values that a difficult situation may afford him. And this decides whether he is worthy of his sufferings or not. ... Such men are not only in concentration camps. Everywhere man is confronted with fate, with the chance of achieving something through his own suffering.

Viktor Frankl - *Man's Search for Meaning*

Frankl is saying that we have to choose how we respond to suffering, to loss, or to grief. We can either wallow in grief and loss, eventually spiraling into self-destructive self-pity, or we can choose to recognize that our loss, our grief has a deeper meaning. When we choose the hope of a brighter new normal, we choose how we respond to the suffering and loss. When we choose our response, we impart meaning and purpose into the suffering.

What do I mean? When I chose to "Flip the Switch" to hope. I chose how I would respond to the grief and loss. Choosing to embrace hope and acceptance of the new normal gave my life and my hope meaning and purpose. When I recognized that purpose, I was able to accept that purpose, to accept my calling.

You can do the same.

CHOOSE HOPE, JOY, AND PURPOSE

What am I saying here? This is where we have a frank conversation. If you have made it through this book, you now know what I lived with for over ten years. Somehow, incredibly, I still have hope in life. I have joy. I have meaning and purpose.

What about you, the reader? Whatever you are going through right now, whatever you have been through, somewhere there is grief and loss. How did you choose to respond? Did you choose hope and meaning, or did you choose to live a life without hope or meaning?

Are you in the middle of grief and loss right now? I empathize with you. Grieve and work through your loss. At some point you will have to decide whether or not to Flip the Switch. I know that it may seem like the the darkness is closing in, but there is light in that darkness. Working through your loss may take time. It may be beneficial to find a support group locally, or to find a trusted friend, or even find a counselor to talk with about your loss. If you have a local faith community, I encourage you to embrace that community.

I understand, and there will be times of darkness in

the future. Sometimes that faint, faint ray of hope from the lighthouse is obscured by clouds of doubt, the fog of fear, or the storms found in the other parts of your life. If you have hope, the beacon is there.

What if you chose to live without hope earlier? Please reconsider. Find help for your grief and loss. It may hurt to become vulnerable enough to ask for help. I urge you to ask. Even the act of asking for help can be the catalyst to Flip the Switch and begin the acceptance and recovery process.

Once you find hope, you will find meaning in your life. Embrace that meaning. Embrace that purpose. And if you get the chance, embrace your humor. Laugh. Feel the joy of life. And occasionally, smile like a pirate.

AFTERWORD

 It has been my observation that the happiest of people, the vibrant doers of the world, are almost always those who are using - who are putting into play, calling upon, depending upon-the greatest number of their God-given talents and capabilities.

John Glenn

As I write this, it is January 8, 2020. One year ago, I lost my leg to an infection that was eating it out. A lot has happened in this first year–and you have read parts of that story. As I sit here typing away on a keyboard, I am filled with all kinds of emotions. I feel grief and sorrow for what happened. Melancholy rears its head as I think about all the low points that I have lived through in the year. Hope and gratefulness also well up in me as I consider my friends, family, and church family, and what a difference they make in my life.

I thought today would be a day when I look back with joy, seeing how far I've come in this journey. Instead, it is a day filled with the other emotions. Instead, here I sit, working on this book. This is the first afterward that I've written before finishing the book, but I think today's timing is important.

I was having a hard time today for most of the day, and didn't even realize what day it was until late in the afternoon. Once I realized that today was January 8th, the crash of emotions made a lot of sense.

What is life like now? I'm getting ready to go in to get fitted for my third socket. The current one is loose, and I can feel it throw off my gait as I walk, giving me uncertainty in my footing. We are in the midst of winter here in Michigan, and even though it has been very mild, I realize that I no longer like winter. Footing is treacherous, and being unable to feel what is going on with the prosthetic as it loses traction truly sucks.

I also found the right underwear. I know, it's a weird thing to be thankful for, but believe me, the right pair of underwear makes all the difference to an above knee (AK) amputee. What makes the right underwear for a guy? Long leg boxer-briefs that are tight enough to hold everything in, and still keep certain anatomical bits tucked up and out of the way. Believe me, having those anatomical bits pinch in between your leg and the socket when you sit down is something you will never forget. You will only do it once.

Small victories and small joys are what can help us through some of the dark periods. The simple joys can really make a difference, providing pools of light when the darkness is most present.

But what keeps me going? Why do I mentor at Mary Free Bed? Why do I speak to amputees when I can?

Hope.

Hope is the key.

Hope in stuff or people from this world will only get you so far. Things break. People let you down. You must find hope in something else. Something higher. I believe the best kind of that hope is in Jesus Christ.

Alexander Pope said that, "hope springs eternal in the human breast." When you have hope in the very creator of the universe, and someone who is the very salvation of humanity, your hope is actually *in* the eternal.

I recommend you live in Hope.

And never forget to smile like a pirate!

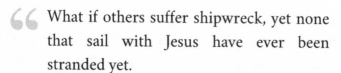

66 What if others suffer shipwreck, yet none that sail with Jesus have ever been stranded yet.

Charles Spurgeon

Fin - February 1, 2020

THANK YOU!

Thank you so much for reading *Smile Like a Pirate! Finding Hope in Loss*. I appreciate your time, and I hope it spoke to you in some way.

This book was a labor of love and pain. If you would like more information about Bryan and his speaking, or would like to invite Bryan to speak, please connect with him on the web or on Facebook.

Online: http://www.bryandonihue.com
Facebook: https://www.facebook.com/authorbryand

If you enjoyed this book, please take the time to add a review on the website of the retailer where you purchased this book.

Also, please feel free to contact me on the website or on Facebook. I love talking to my readers.

Bryan

ABOUT THE AUTHOR

Early in his life, Bryan decided that he would try as many different jobs as possible. Well, it was his high curiosity and low attention span that decided for him. He started in fast food and has worked in sales (retail, used car, business-to-business, door-to-door, credit card processing, vacuum cleaner, and firearms). Bryan has also been a security guard, police  officer, and armored car vault manager. And he was a youth pastor.

Eventually, he decided he'd take the "easy path" and become a writer. He was an idiot. Writing is not easy, but it turned out, he was pretty good at it. People seemed to like his stories, so he kept telling them.

Bryan is a published author (fiction and non-fiction), game designer, graphic artist, web designer, consultant, trainer, ministry leader, and multiple-business owner. He is also happily married to his wife of over 20 years, Christina, and father to six or seven kids, depending on the day. He even sleeps occasionally.

Bryan is currently writing from a hidden bunker in Grand Rapids, Michigan. At least that's what he claims. We know he sits in his home office with a brass plaque that reads "Dungeon" affixed over the door.

https://www.bryandonihue.com

 facebook.com/authorbryand
twitter.com/authorbryand

Made in the USA
Monee, IL
17 August 2021

75731897R00100